W9-AJN-334

DATE DUE

DAHOMEY

THE KINGDOMS OF AFRICA

DAHOMEY

THE WARRIOR KINGS

PHILIP KOSLOW

CHELSEA HOUSE PUBLISHERS · Philadelphia

Frontispiece: A carved wooden lion from the royal palace of Dahomey.
On the Cover: An artist's interpretation of a carved wooden mask from Dahomey; in the background, an 18th-century Dahomean king receives his subjects in a court-yard of the royal palace.

CHELSEA HOUSE PUBLISHERS
Editorial Director   Richard Rennert
Executive Managing Editor   Karyn Gullen Browne
Copy Chief   Robin James
Picture Editor   Adrian G. Allen
Creative Director   Robert Mitchell
Production Manager   Sallye Scott
Art Director   Joan Ferrigno

THE KINGDOMS OF AFRICA
Senior Editor   Martin Schwabacher

Staff for DAHOMEY
Assistant Editor   Catherine Iannone
Editorial Assistant   Erin McKenna
Senior Designer   Cambraia Magalhaes
Picture Researcher   Ellen Barrett Dudley
Cover Illustrator   Bradford Brown

First Printing
1 3 5 7 9 8 6 4 2

Library of Congress Cataloging-in-Publication Data
Koslow, Philip.
  Dahomey: the warrior kings/Philip Koslow
  p. cm.— (The Kingdoms of Africa)
Includes bibliographical references and index.
  ISBN   0-7910-3137-3
        0-7910-3138-1 (pbk)
 1. Benin—History—To 1894—Juvenile literature. I. Title. II. Series
DT541.65.K67 1996
966.9'3—dc20   95-25049

CONTENTS

Titles in
THE KINGDOMS OF AFRICA

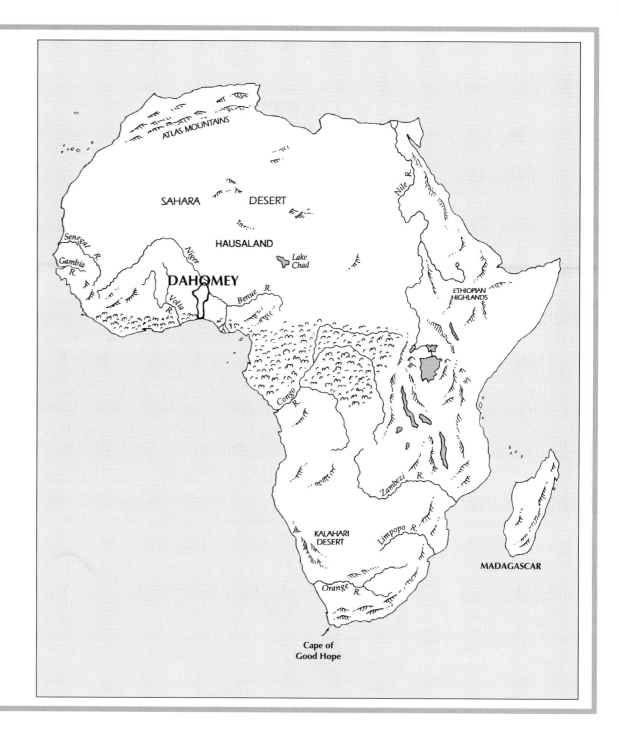

"CIVILIZATION AND MAGNIFICENCE"

O n a sunny morning in July 1796, Mungo Park, a Scottish doctor turned explorer, achieved a major goal of his long and difficult trek through West Africa when he reached the banks of the mighty Niger River. Along the river was a cluster of four large towns, which together made up the city of Segu, the principal settlement of the Bambara people. The sight of Segu dazzled Park as much as the spectacle of the broad, shining waterway. "The view of this extensive city," he wrote, "the numerous canoes upon the river; the crowded population; and the cultivated state of the surrounding country, formed altogether a prospect of civilization and magnificence, which I little expected to find in the bosom of Africa."

Park's account of his journey, *Travels in the Interior Districts of Africa*, became a best-seller in England. But his positive reflections on Africa were soon brushed aside by the English and other Europeans, who were engaged in a profitable trade in slaves along the West African coast and were eventually to carve up the entire continent into colonies. Later explorers such as Richard Burton, who spoke of the "childishness" and "backwardness" of Africans, achieved more lasting fame than did Park, who drowned during a second expedition to Africa in 1806. Thus it is not surprising that 100 years after Park's arrival at Segu, a professor at England's Oxford University could write with bland self-assurance that African history before the arrival of Europeans had been nothing more than "blank, uninteresting, brutal barbarism." The professor's opinion was published

A physical map of Africa indicating the former kingdom of Dahomey.

This carved wooden mask from Dahomey is one of the numerous artworks produced by West Africans before the colonial era.

when the British Empire was at its height, and it represented a point of view that was necessary to justify the exploitation of Africans. If, as the professor claimed, Africans had lived in a state of chaos throughout their history, then their European conquerors could believe that they were doing a noble deed by imposing their will and their way of life upon Africa.

The colonialist view of African history held sway into the 20th century. But as the century progressed, more enlightened scholars began to take a fresh look at Africa's past. As archaeologists (scientists who study the physical remains of past societies) explored the sites of former African cities, they found that Africans had enjoyed a high level of civilization hundreds of years before the arrival of Europeans. In many respects, the kingdoms and cities of Africa had been equal to or more advanced than European societies during the same period.

As early as the 5th century B.C., when ancient Greece was enjoying its Golden Age, West African peoples had developed a highly sophisticated way of life and were producing magnificent works of art. By A.D. 750, ancient Ghana, known as the Land of Gold, emerged as West Africa's first centralized kingdom. When Ghana began to decline in the 12th century, power shifted to the empire of Mali, where the great ruler Mansa Musa became legendary for his wealth, generosity, and refinement. After the 15th century, Mali's grandeur passed to Songhay, which encompassed the great trading cities of Gao, Jenne, and Timbuktu; to the dual kingdom of Kanem-Borno, whose ruling dynasty controlled the shores of Lake Chad for 1,000 years; and to the remarkable fortress kingdoms of Hausaland, whose armored horsemen displayed their valor on the sun-baked plains. All these great nations were located in the heartland of West Africa, the wide savanna that borders the vast Sahara Desert. To a large extent, the savanna kingdoms owed their wealth and grandeur to trade with North Africa and the Middle East. Because of this ever-widening economic and cultural contact, the fame of the Bilad al-Sudan ("land of the black peoples" in Arabic) spread throughout the world.

However, the rich saga of the savanna kingdoms does not represent the entire history of West African achievement. Indeed, much of the savanna's wealth derived from the gold and ivory supplied by the peoples of the lush forest belt that extends along the southern coast of West Africa. Many of the forestland communities, which included Yorubaland, Benin, and Asante, had established themselves as early as the states of the Sudan had, but because of their distant location and rugged terrain they were largely unknown to outsiders until the arrival of European mariners in the 15th century. Once that contact was made, a new era in West African history—often glorious and sometimes tragic—began to unfold. In this developing saga, some of the most dramatic events occurred in one of the region's most powerful and successful nations—the kingdom of Dahomey.

Chapter 1 | THE LEOPARD'S CLAWS

A view of Ganvié, a fishing community on the Dahomean coast. During the 17th century, when the future rulers of Dahomey were still establishing themselves in the north, coastal communities such as Ganvié prospered from trade with visiting European merchants.

In the great days of Dahomey, a crown prince could not take the throne unless he was able to recite the historical chronicles of the nation. These traditions were passed down through the generations by specially trained troubadours, and they are still recounted today. Though the versions of various chroniclers now differ in many details, their histories all begin at the same place—the city of Tado, located just outside the ancient borders of Dahomey, in the present-day nation of Togo.

Long ago, according to the troubadours, the king of Tado was the most powerful ruler in the region. Like most West African monarchs, he had a senior wife and numerous secondary wives. One of these secondary wives mated with a leopard and gave birth to three sons who were raised as the king's children. As the years went by, the king's principal wife bore him no heirs; thus when the king died, one of the leopard's sons was in line to inherit the throne.

The people of Tado would not accept this turn of events. They rose up against the leopard's children, who—after a bloody battle in which they slew many of their enemies—fled south to the region known as Allada. Here, the three brothers became rulers of a kingdom called Aizonu. But with the fierce blood of the leopard flowing in their veins, they could not live at peace with one another. After quarreling bitterly, they decided to go their separate ways. Ajahuto remained in

Allada. Agbanli went farther south and settled on the coast, where he ruled the city of Ajase. The third brother, Agasu, returned to the north and became the mightiest king of all. The clan he founded, known as the Agasuvi, evolved into the ruling family of Dahomey.

Agasu became the *tohwiyo*, or ruling spirit, of his clan. He was worshiped like a supernatural being, and a religious sect devoted to the leopard became a powerful force in Dahomean life. Each succeeding king, upon his coronation, was tattooed by the high priest of the leopard cult: the priest inscribed five tiny marks on the king's temples and three on his forehead, representing the leopard's claws. To this day, members of the Agasuvi clan refuse to eat the meat of the leopard or of any outwardly similar animal, such as the spotted antelope. They also avoid the meat of turtles and shellfish because these creatures are believed to have helped the Agasuvi cross many rivers during their migrations.

Like most African traditions, the popular chronicles of Dahomey's founding describe actual events but interpret them in a poetic manner, reflecting glory upon the past rulers of the nation. Modern scholars studying these traditions believe that the history of Dahomey begins with the founding of Tado around 1300 by peoples migrating from the east, possibly from Yorubaland. At some point in Tado's development, the Agasuvi clan tried to seize the kingship and were expelled. They then traveled south and settled in Allada, where a new dispute within the clan's leading family caused the group to split again. The Agasuvi who migrated north settled in the Abomey region, just east of Tado, gradually intermarrying with local peoples of Yoruba origin and forming a new ethnic group known as the Fon.

Like the other peoples of the region, the Fon continued to speak the language commonly known as Aja. (Aja is also referred to by scholars as Ewe and Gbe.) But their warlike nature set them apart from their neighbors. During their early years they lived a rugged existence, most likely operating as bandits or as mercenaries (soldiers who had no political allegiance but simply fought for any ruler who offered them sufficient pay).

While the Agasuvi were struggling to establish themselves in the north, Allada grew to be the most important of the Aja-speaking states, rivaled only by the coastal kingdom of Whydah. Allada and Whydah benefited greatly from their commerce with European merchants. Europeans began visiting the southern coast of West Africa during the 1470s, bringing goods such as iron, linen, silk, cutlery, and glassware, which they exchanged for gold, ivory, cloth, and slaves.

Whydah and Allada owed much of their prosperity to the slave trade. Their rulers often sold prisoners of war into slavery, exchanging them for firearms, which increased the strength of their armies and enabled them to undertake increasingly successful campaigns against their neighbors. This in turn allowed them to capture more slaves. Soon the slave trade so dominated the economy that the region became known as the Slave Coast.

While these two states were growing rich, the Fon were slowly building their power in the north. Their transformation from hired soldiers to a genuine political force dates from 1625, when a man named Dako became the leader of the Fon and laid the groundwork for a new kingship based in Abomey.

Though they had previously lived in peace with their neighbors, the Fon

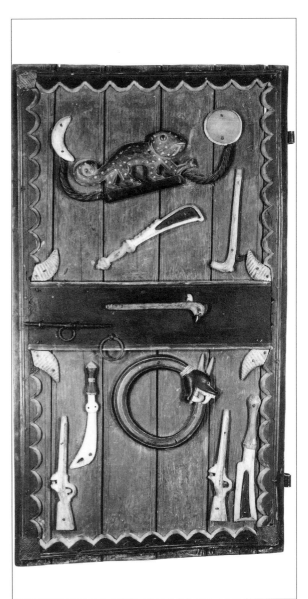

13

The carvings on this door from the royal palace of Dahomey include a leopard (upper panel), the symbol of the ruling Agasuvi clan. The curled-up serpent on the lower panel represents Aida Hwedo, the creative force of the universe.

A densely inhabited village in northwestern Dahomey, where the power of the Agasuvi originally developed. As they gained in strength, the Agasuvi conquered numerous villages and appointed themselves chiefs; these villages later formed the core of the kingdom of Dahomey.

14

now began to seek more land. Armed with slings and clubs, their traditional weapons, small groups of Fon warriors engaged in battle with nearby villages. Time and again, Dako and his warriors proved the stronger force, killing the opposing chief and taking control of his village. By the time of Dako's death in 1650, the Fon controlled an area of about five miles in radius surrounding their original settlement. Dako's achievements were such that upon his death the Fon chiefs readily accepted his son Wegbaja as their king. The royal dynasty of Abomey was born.

Wegbaja reigned from 1650 to 1685 and continued the expansion of Fon power. He levied a special tax on his people and used the proceeds to acquire firearms from the European traders. He also created new methods of warfare, including the technique of surprise attacks launched at dawn, when the enemy was still asleep.

Because of his success in battle and his generosity in handing out spoils to his followers, Wegbaja was also able to increase the power of the kingship. For example, he reserved the right to punish criminals, a power that had previously resided with local chiefs. He also decreed that upon the death of any of his subjects, that person's property would be transferred to the king. The property was immediately returned to the deceased person's heirs, but Wegbaja firmly established the principle that all subjects held their goods by the grace of the king.

The Fon first began to call their kingdom Dahomey during Wegbaja's reign. According to tradition, when Wegbaja decided to build a royal palace in Abomey, he asked a local chief named Dan for a large parcel of land. Dan felt that Wegbaja was demanding far more than he was entitled to, and he replied sarcastically, "Do you want to build in my belly?" (The Aja word for "belly" is *homè*.)

Enraged by this retort, Wegbaja attacked Dan's village and took him captive. When construction of the palace began, Wegbaja slit open Dan's belly, displayed the chief's mutilated body

This elaborately carved wooden stool from Dahomey represents a chief (shaded by umbrella) and a number of his wives and attendants. As Dahomey grew, the kings assumed many of the powers formerly belonging to local chiefs, such as the duty of passing judgment upon lawbreakers.

15

on the foundation, and then built the palace over his remains. To commemorate this incident, the palace was called Danhomè, "in the belly of Dan." The name was eventually applied to the entire kingdom, and the warriors who marched beneath the banners of Dahomey soon became the masters of the Slave Coast.

Chapter 2 | "DAHOMEY IS ITS PEOPLE"

This 18th-century engraving shows a royal audience held by Agaja, king of Dahomey from 1708 to 1732. According to Dahomean custom, officials who wished to address the monarch had to prostrate themselves before the throne and cover their heads with dust.

After each new king of Dahomey took his oath of office, two senior government officials showed him a series of secret rooms in the royal palace. These rooms contained large sacks filled with pebbles, representing the population of Dahomey in different eras. At each stage the sacks grew larger. In the final room, the new king was commanded to kneel, and the elders addressed him in the following terms:

Young man, all your life you have heard "Dahomey, Dahomey," but you have never until today seen the true Dahomey; for Dahomey is its people, and here they are. . . . You must never allow the contents of these sacks to diminish; you must see to it that these pebbles increase in number. You must keep in your mind the small sacks of Wegbaja, and how much larger are those your father has left you. Every year, we will come here with you to count the pebbles, and to see if you have increased their number or reduced it. Young man, rise! We did not give you this thought to discourage you!

Upon assuming the throne, the new king also built his own compound adjacent to the royal palace. Thus the palace grew larger with each succeeding regime, finally covering an area of 15 acres and housing 10,000 people. By expanding his immediate domain, the new king showed that he was prepared to honor the traditional obligation to "make Dahomey greater."

During the 18th century, this command was faithfully carried out by Wegbaja's son Akaba and most spectacularly by his grandson Agaja, who became king of Dahomey in 1708.

Ascending the throne at the age of 19, Agaja was at first content to conquer additional territory in the region of Abomey. By the 1720s, however, Agaja boldly turned his attention to the south. At this time, Whydah and Allada together were dealing about 20,000 slaves a year to Europeans. They were also barring other peoples of the region from taking part in the lucrative coastal trade. According to the account of Archibald Dalzel, whose *History of Dahomy* appeared in 1793, Agaja "sent ambassadors to [Allada] and Whydah, to whose very borders he had already extended his conquests, requesting an open traffic to the seaside, offering at the same time to pay the customary duties. This, as he probably expected, was peremptorily refused; which furnished him with a pretense for obtaining his desire by force."

In addition to gaining access to new markets, Agaja was driven by the desire to reclaim the birthright of the Agasuvi, who had long before been expelled from Allada. Dahomey's forces launched an attack on Allada in 1724 and invaded Whydah in 1726. Given their wealth and the size of their armies, these nations should have been strong enough to repel any invader. However, both Whydah and Allada lacked the efficient political organization and warlike spirit of Dahomey. Dalzel described Whydah's condition in the following terms:

> At this time Whydah was governed by a weak and indolent prince. . . . His indolence and indulgence had swoln him to an enormous size; and, constantly shut up in his seraglio, amongst thousands of women, over whom he asserted the most despotic sway, he vainly imagined his bulk to be the type of his real greatness. Mean while the ministers and caboceers [chiefs] around him, intent on their own private interests, divided the state into a thousand different factions, which added to the natural timidity of the people, the result of plenty, long ease, and inaction, exposed it as a ready prey to any invader.

As a Dahomean detachment approached his territory, the king of Whydah refused to believe that he was in danger. He did not even mobilize his

18

army, believing that Whydah's military reputation would cause the Dahomeans to lose heart. For added measure, he sought the protection of the gods. Like most West Africans, the people of Whydah regarded snakes as sacred beings. A large cave filled with snakes guarded the spot where the Dahomean troops would have to cross the Tori River in order to enter Whydah, and the king assumed that the snakes would find a way to protect his country. His faith was misplaced. Dahomey's soldiers swept across the Tori without any interference, and Agaja was soon master of Whydah. After learning of the destruction visited upon both Whydah and Allada, a number of other rulers quickly submitted to Dahomean rule.

As Agaja was completing his conquests, Europeans were quick to seek his favor. When William Snelgrave, the captain of an English slave ship, sought an audience with Agaja during the campaign against Whydah, he and his party were taken to a large military camp. The installation was filled with thatched huts that reminded the visi-

A map of the kingdom of Dahomey at the height of its power. When each new king took office, he swore an oath to increase the extent and population of the realm.

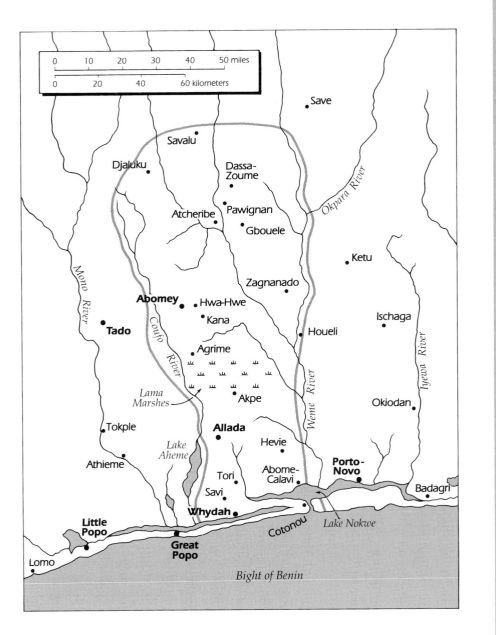

19

20

In this 18th-century engraving, a delegation of European visitors view a procession of the royal wives during the Dahomean festival known as the Annual Customs.

tors of giant beehives, each one providing shelter for 10 to 12 soldiers. As the Englishmen moved through the camp and approached the king's compound, a formidable sight awaited them:

> We were surprised with the sight of forty stout fellows, ranged on both sides of the gate, with fusils [firearms] on their shoulders, and broadswords in their hands; having round their necks strings of dead men's teeth, reaching as low as

their middle, both behind and before, in great quantities. These, we were told, were the King's heroes, or worthies; who, having killed many enemies in battle, were allowed to wear their teeth in this manner, as trophies of their valor: on pain of death, however, if they dared to string one, whose owner had not been killed by their own hands.

The Englishmen were then received by Agaja in a large courtyard within the royal compound. Snelgrave observed that the monarch (now in his late thirties) was "middle-sized and full-bodied." Though Agaja's face bore the scars of smallpox, Snelgrave perceived "something in his countenance very taking, and withal majestic." Agaja was sitting on a golden chair that he had taken from the king of Whydah. As befitted a military commander, he was dressed plainly in a flowing robe that reached to his ankles. His only adornments were a pair of sandals (all other Dahomeans went barefoot) and a European hat. Agaja was surrounded by female attendants who held large umbrellas above his head to shield him from the sun. The women were richly attired, wearing gold armlets and colorful glass beads in their hair.

During the audience, Agaja also received visits from Dahomean officials and military commanders, who threw themselves on the ground at a respectful distance of 20 feet and covered their heads with dust. No one was allowed to speak directly to Agaja; instead they first kissed the ground and then whispered to an elderly attendant, who conveyed their messages to the king. Many of those who came before the king had fought bravely during the campaign, and the attendant returned from Agaja's side to announce the number of captives each man would receive as a reward. The news was then conveyed by an officer to the cheering soldiers waiting outside the gate.

Agaja's personality deeply impressed the Europeans who dealt with him. Summing up his accomplishments, Dalzel praised his "greatness of mind" and concluded that the Dahomean king, "considered as a conqueror, seems little inferior to any other of that class, which has swoln the pages of history. . . . Though rigid to those who opposed his arms, he was mild and generous to those who readily submitted to them. His politeness to Europeans was exemplary; and which, in spite of the injuries he received from a part of them, he honorably continued to the rest." That combination of traits was considered typical by Dahomeans, who liked to say that their kings combined the gentleness of Agasu's human mother with the ferocity of his leopard father.

By extending Dahomey's territory to the coast, Agaja became a revered figure among his countrymen. However, his conquests disrupted farming and trade along the coast, causing European merchants to shy away. Naturally, Dahomey's economy suffered as a result. The task of rebuilding fell to succeeding generations.

21

Chapter 3 | "I AM A WARRIOR"

23

Among the high points of the Annual Customs was the ceremony known as "parading the king's wealth." As the king watched from a huge conical pavilion, his attendants marched past in a procession that lasted for hours; each marcher displayed an object from the royal palace.

Before Agaja died in 1732, he chose his son Zenga to succeed him. The practice of selecting an heir was unusual, and it contributed greatly to Dahomey's consistent success. In most other kingdoms, not only in Africa but throughout the world, the eldest son automatically succeeded his father, whether or not he was fit for the job. But by elevating the ablest of the royal princes to the throne, Dahomeans made sure that they would never suffer for lack of a strong ruler.

Under Dahomean law, however, the will of the monarch was not always supreme. The nation's two highest-ranking court officials, the *migan* and the *meu*, had the power to reject the chosen son if they considered him unfit to lead the nation. For unknown reasons, they rejected Zenga in favor of his brother Tegbesu. Zenga did not take this decision in stride; instead, he rallied a group of supporters and made plans to seize the kingdom. News of the plot reached Tegbesu, and he arrested Zenga and his allies before they could act. Tegbesu had all the plotters beheaded, with the exception of Zenga—Dahomean law forbade the actual spilling of royal blood. Instead, Zenga was sewn up in a hammock and transported to Whydah. There he was placed in a canoe, taken some distance out to sea, and thrown overboard.

Three years later, the meu decided that he and the migan had made a mistake; in his view, Tegbesu was a

24

cruel and tyrannical ruler. Feeling responsible for bringing Tegbesu to the throne, the meu now felt obliged to depose him. After resigning his post, the meu began to raise an army and to plan an assault on Abomey. This was truly a desperate act, for in rebelling the meu had violated the principle of unity that governed many aspects of Dahomean life.

The importance of unity in Dahomey's society is reflected in its religion. According to Dahomean beliefs, the world was created by the god Mawu-Lisa. Mawu-Lisa embodies two distinct personalities, one female (Mawu) and one male (Lisa), thus maintaining the balance of forces that govern the life of humans: night and day, sun and moon, gentleness and domination, rest and labor, peace and conflict.

When Mawu-Lisa finished creating the world, she/he created distinct domains for her/his children—the gods known in Dahomey as the major *vodun*. These vodun in turn governed a host of lesser vodun, all of whom played a direct role in human affairs. Thus the activities of the gods were identical to the procedures followed by the rulers of Dahomey. The heads of families, the leaders of clans, and the

chiefs of villages had roles similar to the various vodun: each commanded his own sphere but was also responsible to a higher authority and ultimately to the king. Thus everyone lived within a network of carefully defined powers and obligations.

On all levels of society, Dahomeans confirmed their unity through a ritual known as "drinking the earth." The actual beverage they imbibed in this ceremony—a mysterious mixture of water, kola nut juice, gin, palm oil, chicken blood, and (supposedly) the innards of those who had offended the vodun—was prepared by priests who supervised the worship of the various vodun.

The ritual first arose among groups of hunters and farmers and was then adopted by villages wishing to form alliances for mutual protection. It was later employed by Dahomean kings to cement their alliances with important chiefs and officials. By drinking the earth with the king these men became his "brothers" and thus owed him as much loyalty as they owed their own families. Those who drank the earth and then broke their oath might be possessed by demons who would cause their eyes to protrude from their heads

(Continued on page 29)

DAHOMEAN SCULPTURE

Like many African kingdoms, Dahomey organized craftspeople such as wood-carvers and sculptors into specialized guilds that were closed to outsiders. In Abomey, Dahomey's capital, each guild occupied a specific neighborhood. In many cases, artists were supported by the king, who commissioned works for his private collection.

This lion from the collection of King Behanzin was carved out of wood and then covered with thin sheets of beaten gold and silver. The metal plates were then attached to the body of the sculpture with silver nails.

Dahomean artists created this statue, approximately five feet high, from sheets of iron obtained in trade with European merchants. The figure represents Gu, the Dahomean god associated with war and ironworking.

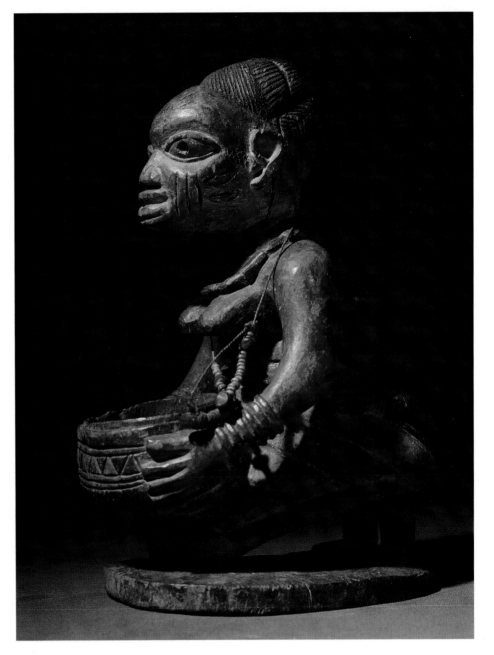

This wood carving depicts a woman with a calabash, a vessel used to hold food or water. The decoration of calabashes was a time-honored and popular art in Dahomean villages, and the objects were often exchanged as gifts between lovers.

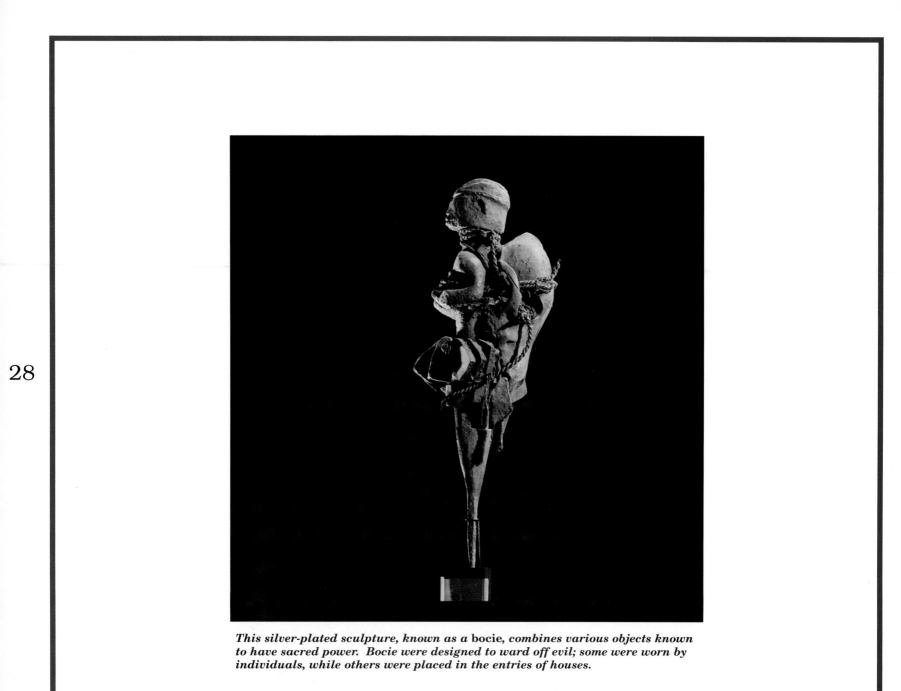

This silver-plated sculpture, known as a bocie, combines various objects known to have sacred power. Bocie were designed to ward off evil; some were worn by individuals, while others were placed in the entries of houses.

(Continued from page 24)

and make them jabber incoherently or utter animal cries; those who managed to escape immediate punishment would pass on their shame to their descendants, a terrible fate for Africans to contemplate.

This ceremony reinforced the spiritual power of the king. Just as the soul of each human being belonged to Mawu-Lisa, the life of a Dahomean belonged to his king. As a Dahomean commander told the English slave trader Robert Norris later in Tegbesu's reign, "I think of the king, and then I dare engage five of the enemy myself. . . . My head belongs to the king, not to myself; if he pleases to send for it, I am ready to resign it; or if it is shot through in battle, it makes no difference to me; I am satisfied, so that it is in the service of my king."

Thus it was not surprising that in the face of the meu's revolt, Dahomey's army commander and a number of veteran officers rallied to their king, enabling him to retain the throne. Though Tegbesu executed the rebellious meu, he showed exceptional clemency to the man's family, even appointing the deceased meu's brother to succeed him in office.

After surviving the meu's rebellion, Tegbesu had to confront a serious challenge from the east. Fattened by its recent conquests, Dahomey was now a rich prize for the rulers of Oyo, the most powerful of the Yoruba states. In 1738, Oyo's cavalry swept across the plains into Dahomey, plundering the land until they reached the very gates of Abomey. The Dahomeans defended their territory fiercely, inflicting heavy casualties upon the Oyo, but Tegbesu was finally forced to flee Abomey and take refuge with his wives in a secret hiding place.

As soon as the Dahomeans knew their king was safe they retreated, abandoning Abomey to the Oyo. The conquerors occupied the city until the approach of the summer rains, when they returned home to plant their crops. But the following year the Oyo invaded once again. Realizing that they could not repel the Oyo, the Dahomeans chose to fall back, allowing the invaders to plunder until they had had their fill. The yearly incursions continued until 1747, when Tegbesu signed a peace treaty with Oyo that called for a yearly tribute payment of slaves and money.

Though the tribute payments were undoubtedly galling to a warlike people

29

such as the Dahomeans, their nation continued to flourish. According to an Englishman who visited the region during the 1740s, "The natives were so industrious, that no place which was thought fertile, could escape being planted, though even within the hedges that enclose their villages and dwelling places; and they were so very anxious in this particular, that, the next day, after they had reaped, they always sowed again, without allowing the land any time to rest."

The Dahomeans were able to plant so many crops in rapid succession because their soil was exceptionally fertile, especially in the wide plateau that rose gently from the coast to Abomey. Farmers grew a wide variety of crops, including such native plants as yams, millet, and cotton. The Dahomeans also planted maize, manioc, beans, peanuts, and tobacco, which had been brought from the Americas by European traders. In the villages, houses were commonly surrounded by fruit trees that yielded bananas, oranges, lemons, avocados, papayas, and pineapples. Nearly every family raised chickens, pigs, sheep, and goats, which were often allowed to run free. Along the coast, oysters,

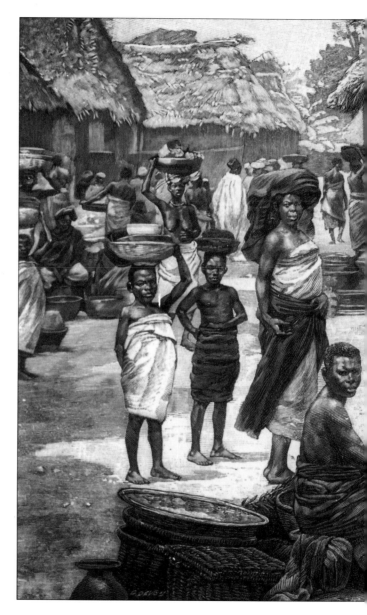

30

A Dahomean market, depicted in a 19th-century engraving. Markets were held every four to five days throughout Dahomey and played a vital role in the life of the people. Most of the goods were transported and sold by women, who sometimes journeyed overnight to reach the market from their homes.

31

32

shrimp, and many varieties of fish were caught by casting nets from canoes or setting traps across lagoons and inlets.

The majority of Dahomey's population was engaged in farming, which occupied them for nine months of the year. (Only during the dry season between January and March, when the cold wind known as the harmattan blew from the north, did farmers abandon their fields and turn to other pursuits.) Each day farmers would rise at dawn and work until late morning. When the heat became truly intense, the farmers would take a three-hour siesta, then continue working until nightfall. Though some chiefs and other wealthy citizens were exempt from all forms of labor, Dahomeans prided themselves on their self-reliance and industry. In the Abomey region, the saying arose that "every Dahomean must know three things well: how to cut a field, how to build a wall, and how to roof a house."

One of the most important features of Dahomean life was the *dokpwe*, a cooperative work group that performed jobs too big for an individual to handle alone. Beyond its immediate function, the dokpwe represented the unity and power of Dahomey. For this reason,

every able-bodied man in a village was expected to join the dokpwe. Anyone who failed to do so was likely to become an outcast; his wives would leave him and his relatives would disown him. The leader of the dokpwe, known as the *dokpwegan*, had great influence in the village and also presided at funerals. Anyone who passed a working dokpwe was obliged to kneel down before the dokpwegan, explain what activity he was engaged in, and ask permission to continue on his way. Even the king was not exempt from this obligation, and during the 19th century King Glele had to pay a fine after passing a dokpwe without observing the proper courtesy.

Though much of the heavy labor fell to men, women also played an important role in the economy. Markets were held every four or five days throughout Dahomey, and it was the women's job to bring produce and cooked food to the market, where many of them had their own individual stalls. Women were sometimes so busy with marketing that they did not have time to cook for their families; instead they bought prepared food at the market and took it home. This practice also enhanced the sense of

A group of captives wait to be taken from the West African coast to a slave ship. According to Dahomean law, only prisoners of war could be sold to European slave traders; for this reason among others, the Dahomean army mounted frequent campaigns against neighboring peoples.

unity among Dahomeans, as the women were, in effect, feeding one another's families.

In addition to food, the markets provided handicrafts such as pottery (almost always made by women) and various European goods from the coast, including knives, jewelry, liquor, firearms, soap, and matches. Shoppers usually paid for their purchases with cowries, the small white shells used as currency in much of West Africa. The smallest unit of currency was the toque, a string of 40 cowries; the next highest was the galline (200), followed by a head (2,000), and a sack of 10 heads (20,000). European merchants were always amazed by the speed and dexterity with which African traders could count out tens of thousands of cowries, keeping all the sums in their heads.

Throughout Dahomey's history, the nation's prosperity depended primarily on the slave trade. Between 1690 and 1850 the Slave Coast was at its peak of operation, exporting more than 1.5 million slaves in all, the great majority of them shipped to the sugar plantations of Brazil and the Caribbean islands. According to law, no Dahomean citizen could be sold into slavery. Slaves were drawn mostly from neighboring Aja- and Yoruba-speaking peoples who were captured in wars and slave raids. Like the rulers of Whydah and Allada before them, Dahomean kings and chiefs considered it their privilege to dispose of these captives as they wished. They most likely did not realize that the loss of able-bodied workers was weakening Africa and paving the way for eventual European domination. Their overriding concern was to enhance the glory of their own nation.

The benefits of Dahomey's slave trade were obvious. When Robert Norris visited Abomey in 1772, he found Tegbesu's royal court in a flourishing state. Norris arrived during the Annual Customs, the great national celebration that often lasted three months. At this time, Abomey contained about 24,000 inhabitants. Like many West African communities, the city consisted of numerous family compounds, each separated from the others by a low mud wall. According to Norris, Tegbesu had two residences inside the city and another on the outskirts. The outer walls of these dwellings were decorated with human skulls, all of them taken from enemies slain in battle.

The ceremonies of the Annual Customs were calculated to inspire awe, both in Dahomeans and in foreign visitors, and to confirm the king's supreme power. In the midst of numerous public entertainments, the king received delegates from each village in Dahomey, collecting tax payments but also dispensing gifts. Everyone who had done service during the year received a reward in the form of cowries, textiles, or wives chosen from the thousands of women housed in the royal palace. (Each village was expected to provide a number of young men for the army and a number of young women for the royal harem.)

34

This engraving shows the king of Dahomey leading a group of warriors into combat. Traditionally, the king paid a bonus to every soldier who returned from battle with prisoners or severed heads.

35

Like many other features of Dahomean society, the king's bestowal of wives increased the status of the crown at the expense of traditional family alliances—many prominent families were in effect created by the king at the Annual Customs and thus owed him a special allegiance.

During the festivities, the king also exercised his power to pass judgment upon criminals, who were paraded before the throne to receive their sentences. During the 18th century, the beheading of condemned criminals and selected prisoners of war was a major feature of the Annual Customs.

36

The executions had a religious as well as a political function. Dahomeans believed that their deceased ancestors became vodun, and as such they were worshiped like the other gods. The public executions enabled the king to honor his own forebears by "watering their graves," sending them fresh servants to attend to their needs in the other world.

During several visits to the royal court, Norris struck up a friendship with Kpengla, Tegbesu's eldest son. Tegbesu himself was forced to decline all food at public banquets; the kings of Dahomey never allowed their subjects to see them eating or sleeping, thus reinforcing the idea that they were somehow more than human. Kpengla was under no such restriction and happily accepted roast chicken and other treats from Norris's table. In 1774, however, when Tegbesu died and Kpengla succeeded to the throne, the happy-go-lucky youngster quickly proved to be the equal of his father in warlike severity. Kpengla became known to his subjects as the Male Oyster, earning this nickname because he was equally hard to crack.

Shortly after taking the throne, Kpengla dispatched his troops to the coastal lagoons, where the remnants of Whydah's people had settled after being displaced by the Dahomeans. Two brothers, Eyi and Abavo, were vying for the throne of Whydah, and Kpengla sided with Eyi. Abavo, known as the Swamp Dog, proved a difficult opponent, as his men employed their swift canoes to elude Dahomey's superior forces. But after a long campaign that lasted well into 1775, Abavo surrendered in order to save his followers from annihilation, and he was soon beheaded by Kpengla.

When Norris visited Kpengla at the end of the year, he gained a vivid picture of the Male Oyster's temperament:

At our first interview, he asked me if I had ever seen Abavou. On replying that I had not, he added, "Then you shall now." . . . Some women, to whom he gave directions about it, soon returned from an inner apartment of the palace, carrying a wide, shallow, brass vessel, that contained a large bundle. . . . This bundle was composed of various folds of cloth, the uppermost of cotton; within them were several silk wrappers, which being removed, Abavou's head made its appearance, lying in a china basin. It was in perfect preservation, as dry as an Egyptian mummy, and

(Continued on page 41)

PAGEANTS IN CLOTH

The creation of appliqué cloths, in which cutout figures are sewn to a fabric background, was one of the most distinctive features of Dahomean art. Appliqué workers designed colorful cloths for a wide variety of patrons, including the royal family, religious societies, military units, and village chiefs.

This cloth depicts a desperate struggle between a lion and a female Dahomean warrior, identified by the crocodile insignia on her cap. The task of hunting elephants was often given to female warriors, exposing them to all the dangers lurking in the wilds.

This cloth depicts a series of Dahomean religious ceremonies designed to ward off evil spirits. The serpentlike figure at the top may represent Aida-Hwedo, the creative force of the universe.

In this appliqué cloth from the royal palace, King Behanzin (lower left, in the guise of a leopard) tries to defend his people against a lion and a group of enemy soldiers.

39

40

This embroidered cotton tunic from the modern nation of Benin (formerly Dahomey) exemplifies the skillful weaving and cloth making that West Africans have practiced for centuries.

(Continued from page 36)

the hair smartly dressed. "That is the fellow," said the king, "who gave me so much trouble." I replied, you seem to take good care of him, now you have him. "Yes," said he, "I am a warrior myself, and should I fall into the enemy's hands, could wish to be treated with that decency, of which I set the example."

In addition to his prowess in war, Kpengla took measures to increase the efficiency of the government and to promote trade. He improved the roads throughout the kingdom and filled in some of the worst stretches of the Lama Marshes, a swampy tract that lay between Abomey and the coast. He also broke with tradition by personally trading in slaves, thus directly increasing the revenues of the crown. When he died in 1789, he left his son Agonglo a strong and wealthy kingdom. By this time, however, the world was slowly becoming a perilous place for monarchs. The American colonies had shaken off the yoke of King George III of Britain, and the French Revolution was under way. The victorious forces of liberty in France, after beheading King Louis XVI, would soon abolish slavery in all French possessions. Within a few years the other European powers, as well as the emerging United States, would also move to end the operations of slave traders such as Robert Norris. The kings of Dahomey would soon confront a host of new challenges.

41

Chapter 4 | "CONQUER OR DIE"

A group of female Dahomean soldiers, popularly known as Amazons, photographed during the early 20th century. Though officially numbered among the royal wives, the Amazons became an essential part of Dahomey's army during the 19th century, often out-performing male troops in battle.

As the 19th century began, it appeared that Dahomey might join the list of nations convulsed by revolution. Royal revenues suffered from a slump in the coastal trade, and the new king, Adanzan, made up the difference by increasing taxes on wealthy Dahomeans. This was not a popular policy, and a number of chiefs eventually threw their support to Adanzan's brother Gezo. In 1818, Gezo seized the throne, and a Dahomean king was deposed for the first time in the nation's history. Adanzan was confined to the royal palace for the rest of his life, and the legend arose that he had become a vodun while still alive.

The advent of Gezo revived Dahomey's fortunes. A broad-shouldered man standing more than six feet tall, Gezo won more battles than any ruler since Agaja. He is credited with conquering 126 separate towns in Mahi country (just north of Abomey) and with bringing all the Mahi people under Dahomean control. Most important, he freed Dahomey from its shameful subjugation to Oyo. By the 1820s, the Oyo empire was beginning to crumble, and Gezo took advantage of the situation by refusing to make the yearly tribute payment. When it became clear that Oyo's forces were incapable of punishing Dahomey for this lapse, Gezo went on the offensive and conquered a number of the western Yoruba peoples who had previously been under Oyo's sway.

Under Gezo's command, Dahomey's army adopted a practice that made it unique in the history of West Africa—the use of female soldiers. Popularly

44

known among Europeans as Amazons, after the legendary female warriors celebrated in ancient Greek myths, these women originally belonged to the royal harem and were chosen for service as the king's personal bodyguards. Deciding that the Amazons were an untapped resource, Gezo increased their numbers and placed them on an equal footing with the male troops.

When the British naval officer Frederick Forbes visited Abomey in 1849 and 1850, he noted that of 7,000 soldiers taking part in a military review, nearly 3,000 were women. All of them were housed in the royal palace, and they were accorded many of the same privileges as the king's other wives—for example, servants walked ahead of them in the street to warn everyone of their approach, because ordinary men were not supposed to set eyes on the king's wives. Though the Amazons accepted this gesture of honor, they had little in common with the other royal wives. Forbes reported hearing one of their officers proclaim, "As the blacksmith takes an iron bar and by fire changes its fashion, so have we changed our nature. We are no longer women, we are men."

The dress of the Amazons was identical to that of male troops. They wore blue-and-white-striped cotton tunics, knee-length cotton trousers, and close-fitting white caps bearing the insignia of their regiments, such as a crocodile, a cross, or a crown. The officers were set apart by coral necklaces, and all the Amazons carried small whips in addition to their long-barreled muskets, which they fired with great skill during military displays.

While in Abomey, Forbes attended a ceremony at which the king reviewed all the Amazon regiments. The first to step forward was the formidable Fanti company, whose duties included elephant hunting. These women, toughened by the rigors of outdoor life, were the elite corps of Amazons. Parading before the king, they celebrated their recent battles against the Mahi and Atakpame. They were especially proud of their role in the assault on Atakpame, pointing out that in this action the male troops had run away while they themselves had stormed the ramparts and had taken the city:

"Have we not conquered," [one officer] exclaimed, "all the province of Mahee? So we will always conquer or die." Then a second officer stepped forward and said: "When the Attahpahms heard we were advancing, they ran away. If we go to war, and any return not conquerors, let them die. If I retreat, my life is at the king's mercy. Whatever the town to be attacked, we will conquer, or bury ourselves in its ruins." . . . After saluting the male and female courts, one of the amazons said: "I have no promises to make: as I have behaved and will behave, so I am ready to be judged: let my actions prove me!" Then another added: "By the king's offspring I swear never to retreat." Whilst a third continued: "War is our great friend; without it there is no cloth, no armlets; let us to war, and conquer or die."

With such warlike zeal at his command, Gezo had no difficulty securing the continued loyalty of Dahomey's chiefs. However, the world outside Dahomey continued to change rapidly. By 1815, all the nations of Europe as well as the United States had officially abolished the transatlantic slave trade. Though this measure did not put an end to the selling of human beings, it did change its focus. The South American nation of Brazil now became Dahomey's major customer, paying such high prices for slaves that its

A portrait of Gezo, king of Dahomey between 1818 and 1859. Though Dahomey remained a powerful nation during Gezo's reign, the king attempted to prepare his people for future challenges by making far-reaching reforms.

45

business made up for the overall decline of the slave trade. Brazil assumed such a prominent role in Dahomey's affairs that one Brazilian, Francisco da Souza, actually became

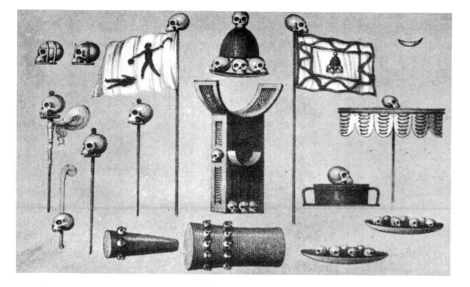

A collection of objects from the royal court of Dahomey testifies to the warlike traditions of the Dahomean state.

46

an official in Gezo's court and had the responsibility of dealing with all European visitors. The son of a Portuguese father and an African mother, da Souza lived like a Dahomean chief, presiding over a large plantation and possessing numerous wives. At the same time, he was thoroughly conversant with European culture, and visitors praised him as a man of great charm and intelligence.

Da Souza's diplomatic skills were highly valuable to Gezo because Dahomey was under considerable pressure to end the slave trade. When Commander Forbes visited Dahomey, for example, his main purpose was to convince Gezo to abandon slaving in favor of other economic pursuits. Throughout the coastal regions of West Africa, the trade in palm oil was rapidly replacing slavery as the focus of European interest. Extracted from the nuts of the palm trees growing abundantly throughout the region, palm oil was widely used in Europe to lubricate machinery and to manufacture soap, candles, and margarine. Forbes argued that Gezo should not be diminishing the population of the coast by selling slaves to the Brazilians; instead, he should be building up the population so that more labor would be available for the palm oil industry and other agricultural ventures.

Gezo was sympathetic to Forbes's arguments and treated him and his party with great consideration. However, he was well aware that his nation's prosperity was still tied to the slave trade. If he put an end to slaving, Dahomey would need time to cultivate more oil palms, and meanwhile Gezo would have to face the wrath of wealthy citizens who were suffering a decline in income.

Despite his rebuff of the British requests, Gezo clearly agreed that large-scale agriculture was the best

Dahomean workers crush palm nuts before extracting the kernels and boiling them down to produce palm oil. During the 19th century, palm oil became West Africa's most valuable export, gradually supplanting the declining slave trade.

47

hope for Dahomey's future. While allowing the slave trade to continue, he did everything possible to increase the nation's agricultural output. He encouraged the planting of new types of corn and offered land to liberated slaves who were returning to Africa from Brazil. Instead of executing prisoners of war, he put them to work on plantations throughout the kingdom.

In general, Gezo faced the classic dilemma of a farseeing monarch who realizes that his country must change in order to survive, but who also knows that challenging the old ways may cause his own downfall. As a result, he did his best to compromise and achieved only part of what he originally envisioned. When Gezo died of smallpox in 1858, he was mourned as a great king, and he is still credited with bringing Dahomey to the height of its glory. But without fundamental change, that glory was to prove fragile in the dangerous political currents of the late 19th century.

Chapter 5 | THE LEOPARD AT BAY

West African textile workers produce cotton cloth at their looms. Beginning in the 19th century, Dahomean craftspeople made dazzling appliqué cloths celebrating the achievements of monarchs and the events of everyday life.

Gezo's son Glele was determined to carry on the warlike exploits of the leopard clan, despite the continued urging of Europeans that he turn Dahomey into a peace-loving agricultural state. During his reign (1858–89), Dahomey's armies mounted 13 separate expeditions against 53 towns, taking thousands of prisoners. These conquests ensured that Glele, who resembled his father in physical stature, would be equally revered throughout his kingship.

Though the kings of Dahomey were exceptional—even among West African monarchs—for their pursuit of power and conquest, they did not ignore other, more refined pursuits. Indeed, the power of the monarchy stimulated the arts to a high degree. Like many other powerful rulers, such as the pharaohs of ancient Egypt and the princes of Renaissance Italy, the kings of Dahomey commissioned numerous artworks to glorify their rule.

Nearly all of Dahomey's leading artists and craftspeople lived in Abomey, where they were organized into guilds based upon family ties. Young artists followed their elders in practicing various skills, such as wood carving, brass casting, or designing appliqué cloths, and the guilds were closed to outsiders. Each guild had its own ward near the royal palace. In addition, Dahomey's artists were all full-time professionals; the support of the king relieved them of the burden of earning a living through farming or other occupations.

50

Among the most remarkable Dahomean artworks are the dramatic appliqué cloths and giant umbrellas (7 to 12 feet in diameter) created by the guild of needleworkers. The figures on the cloths and umbrellas illustrated well-known proverbs and represented the king's accomplishments. (Each king had his own insignia: Gezo was the buffalo, Glele the elephant, Glele's son Behanzin the shark.) In Dahomey, the possession of a personal umbrella was a great point of honor. Ordinary citizens were not allowed to use them, and young chiefs were obliged to use plain white umbrellas; only when they had distinguished themselves in battle could they commission artists to adorn their umbrellas with scenes of their exploits.

During the Annual Customs, one of the major ceremonies was known as "parading the king's wealth." This consisted of a massive procession in which hundreds of people took part, each carrying a precious object belonging to the king. Among the articles on display were metal sculptures representing a wide variety of subjects, ranging from wild animals to scenes of everyday life. Some of these sculptures were truly spectacular, such as a six-foot-tall silver stork, a five-foot silver candelabrum in the shape of a tree, and a giant silver skull, all of them made by the royal silversmith. Dahomey's sculptors achieved the same level of quality as the artists of Benin, Asante, and Yorubaland, whose sculptures

This 19th-century statue portrays King Glele of Dahomey in the form of a lion. Each Dahomean king was represented by an animal endowed with strength, courage, and ferocity.

rank among the world's great art-works, but because the kings did not allow these works to leave the country, they were little known to the outside world until recent times.

Though Dahomey's most lavish artifacts belonged exclusively to the king, the common people also engaged in decorative arts. In every Dahomean village, craftspeople carved designs into calabashes, the vessels used in everyday life to hold food and water. (The carvers normally used plants and animals for their designs. According to Dahomean beliefs, artists who depicted human figures could be prevented by the gods from having children.) The carved calabashes were never put to household use but were exchanged as gifts, especially between people in love. Each design illustrated a proverb. For example, a suitor might send his beloved a calabash with an engraving of a snake, a knife, and a dish containing the snake's severed head: this indicated that the man was ready to take on any rival for the woman's love. The depiction of a long-billed bird spearing a fish conveyed the idea that lovers should be joined as easily as the bird swallowed its prey.

However successful and cultivated

A calabash bearing the image of a warrior. Carved calabashes were the favorite art form of Dahomey's common people, and lovers often exchanged them as gifts.

51

his kingdom might be, Glele could not prevent the increasing interference of Europeans in West African affairs. In earlier times, Europeans had been content to buy slaves and sail away; they were now pressing for control of the palm oil trade and other profitable ventures, and their increasing military

Dahomean troops fire upon the Topaz, *a French gunboat, during a battle in 1892. At this time, the French were conducting an all-out campaign to conquer Dahomey.*

52

strength made them harder to withstand. Glele managed to stave off the ambitions of the British and Portuguese, but the French were more tenacious. They were well established at Dahomey's southern ports, and they convinced a number of local chiefs to sign treaties granting them greater commercial privileges. In 1889, the French asserted their rights under these treaties and demanded that Glele give up the customs revenue at the major port of Cotonou in return for a yearly pension. Glele refused to do so, indicating that he did not recognize the treaties and that he had beheaded the chiefs who had signed them.

Glele died that same year, and

Behanzin inherited the conflict over Cotonou. Refusing to back down, he launched several attacks against the port, all of which were repulsed by the French. Finally, in 1892, French forces took the offensive and mounted an assault on Abomey. Despite the discipline and valor of the Dahomean troops, their antiquated muskets were no match for the rapid-fire rifles, machine guns, and heavy artillery of the enemy. When they realized that Abomey was destined to fall into French hands, the Dahomeans set fire to their capital, and Behanzin went into hiding. There followed a long period of negotiation, and finally, in January 1894, Behanzin agreed to step down and go into exile on the island of Martinique, a French possession in the Caribbean Sea. On his way to the boat that would take him from his kingdom, Behanzin followed an ancient Dahomean tradition by improvising a song about his enemies, expressing his scorn for them and his defiance of their power.

In 1904, Dahomey was incorporated into the larger colony known as French West Africa. Several times over the next decade the Dahomeans rose up in revolt, but each time the French

53

A portrait of King Behanzin, who led Dahomey's fight against French domination during the early 1890s. Following the defeat of his forces, Behanzin spent the rest of his life in exile on the French island of Martinique in the Caribbean Sea.

Having achieved independence in 1960, the nation of Dahomey became the Republic of Benin in 1975.

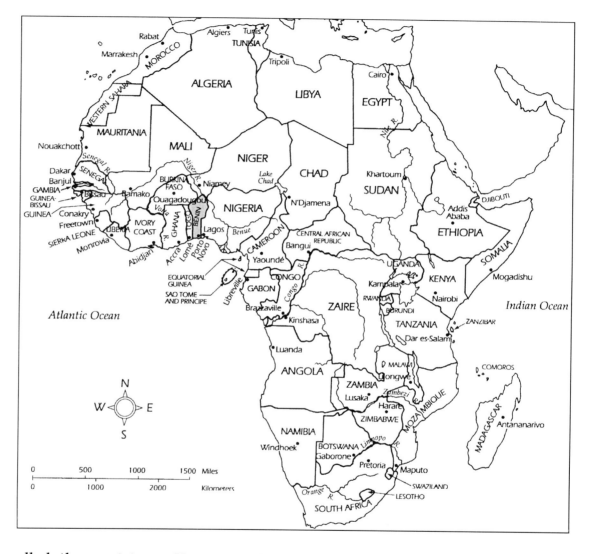

54

quelled the uprising. However, after World War II ended in 1945, the drive for freedom all over Africa became irresistible. The French were forced to allow the formation of political parties in Dahomey, and under the leadership of such men as Hubert Maga, Dahomeans mounted a powerful independence movement. Finally, on January 15, 1960, the modern nation of Dahomey was born.

In 1975, Dahomey changed its name to Benin. The country now has a population of more than 3 million, up from 200,000 during the heyday of the Dahomean empire. Gezo's plans have finally reached fruition, as almost all of Benin's gross national product is derived from the palm oil industry.

Though the Dahomean monarchy no longer exists, the Fon and the other Aja-speaking peoples that make up the bulk of Benin's population continue to live under their traditional chiefs, and most still observe their age-old religions. (In many cases, Africans who have adopted Christianity and Islam also worship traditional gods.) These beliefs have had an influence that goes far beyond the borders of Benin. Because so many captives were shipped from Dahomey to Brazil and the Caribbean, their religious beliefs took root in the Americas. In parts of Brazil, for example, religious services are still conducted in Aja, and the dances accompanying religious rituals are purely African.

Perhaps the best-known example of Dahomean religious influence resides in Haiti's vodun cults, popularly known as voodoo. The dreaded zombies of Haitian belief—the living dead—derive from the Dahomean concept of multiple souls. One of these souls, which the Haitians call the *gros-bon-ange* (the great good angel), animates the body; if a person dies and the gros-bon-ange is captured by a *bocor,* a master of the evil arts, that soul will walk the earth and do the bocor's bidding. Proper religious observance, in which souls are entrusted to vodun priests, can prevent such frightful occurrences.

In all parts of the world, those who follow ancient Dahomean beliefs pay special attention to the souls of their ancestors. This sense of continuity has enabled the present-day citizens of Benin and all people of Dahomean descent to meet the challenges of modern life and to strive for a better future.

CHRONOLOGY

c. 1300   Aja-speaking peoples establish the kingdom of Tado; Agasuvi clan, future rulers of Dahomey, eventually branch off from royal family of Tado and form new ethnic group known as the Fon

1470s   Europeans begin visiting the southern coast of West Africa and establish trade relations with Africans

c. 1600   Transatlantic slave trade develops along the West African coast; Whydah and Allada prosper as slave-dealing states

c. 1625   Fon begin to expand their territory under the leadership of Dako, who founds the royal dynasty of Dahomey

1650–85   Reign of Wegbaja as king of Dahomey; Wegbaja builds up the nation's military forces, increases the power of the kingship, and builds a royal palace in Abomey

1724–27   Led by King Agaja, Dahomeans conquer Whydah and Allada, becoming the major power on the Slave Coast

1732   Tegbesu becomes king of Dahomey

1738   Oyo launches invasion of Dahomey and occupies Abomey; incursions are repeated yearly

1747   Tegbesu signs treaty with Oyo, agreeing to yearly tribute payment in return for peace

1774–89	Reign of Kpengla as king of Dahomey; Kpengla mounts numerous successful military campaigns against Dahomey's neighbors
1815	European nations outlaw the transatlantic slave trade; Brazilians become Dahomey's principal partners in the slave trade
1818–58	Reign of Gezo; Gezo ends tribute payments to Oyo; subdues the neighboring states of Mahi and Atakpame as well as the western Yoruba; increases number and role of female soldiers (Amazons) in Dahomean army; attempts to build up agriculture as alternative to slave trade
1858–89	Reign of Glele; Dahomeans conquer 53 more towns and maintain their supreme power on the Slave Coast
1885	European powers agree to divide Africa into colonies; France begins to assert claims to Dahomean ports
1889	Behanzin becomes king of Dahomey and defies French demands
1892	French forces attack Abomey; Dahomeans burn their capital as Behanzin goes into hiding
1894	Behanzin surrenders to the French and goes into permanent exile
1904	Dahomey becomes part of French West Africa
1960	Dahomey achieves independence
1975	Dahomean government changes the nation's name to Benin

FURTHER READING

Akinjogbin, I. A. *Dahomey and Its Neighbors, 1708–1818*. Cambridge: Cambridge University Press, 1967.

Argyle, William J. *The Fon of Dahomey*. Oxford: Clarendon Press, 1966.

Bosman, William. *A New and Accurate Description of the Coast of Guinea*. Reprint of the 1705 edition. London: Cass, 1967.

Curtin, Philip D., ed. *Africa Remembered: Narratives by West Africans from the Era of the Slave Trade*. Madison: University of Wisconsin Press, 1967.

Dalzel, Archibald. *The History of Dahomy*. Reprint of the 1793 edition. London: Cass, 1967.

Davidson, Basil. *Africa in History*. Rev. ed. New York: Collier, 1991.

———. *The African Slave Trade*. Rev. ed. Boston: Little, Brown, 1980.

Davidson, Basil, with F. K. Buah and the advice of J. F. A. Ajayi. *A History of West Africa, 1000–1800*. New rev. ed. London: Longmans, 1977.

Forbes, Frederick E. *Dahomey and the Dahomans*. 2 vols. Reprint of the 1851 edition. London: Cass, 1966.

Herskovits, Melville J. *Dahomey: An Ancient West African Kingdom*. 2 vols. Evanston, IL: Northwestern University Press, 1967.

Hull, Richard W. *African Cities and Towns Before the European Conquest*. New York: Norton, 1976.

Law, Robin. *The Slave Coast of West Africa*. Oxford: Oxford University Press, 1991.

Lombard, Jacques. "The Kingdom of Dahomey." In *West African Kingdoms in the Nineteenth Century*, edited by Darryll Forde and P. M. Kaberry. Oxford: Oxford University Press, 1967.

McEvedy, Colin. *The Penguin Atlas of African History*. New York: Penguin, 1980.

Manning, Patrick. *Slavery, Colonialism, and Economic Growth in Dahomey, 1640–1960*. Cambridge: Cambridge University Press, 1982.

Norris, Robert. *Memoirs of the Reign of Bossa Ahadee, King of Dahomy*. Reprint of the 1789 edition. London: Cass, 1968.

Park, Mungo. *Travels in the Interior Districts of Africa*. Reprint of the 1799 edition. New York: Arno Press/New York Times, 1971.

Ronen, Dov. *Dahomey Between Tradition and Modernity*. Ithaca, NY: Cornell University Press, 1975.

Simpson, George Eaton. *Black Religions in the New World*. New York: Columbia University Press, 1978.

Smith, Robert. *Warfare and Diplomacy in Pre-Colonial West Africa*. 2nd ed. Madison: University of Wisconsin Press, 1989.

Snelgrave, William. *A New Account of Some Parts of Guinea and the Slave Trade*. Reprint of the 1734 edition. London: Cass, 1971.

UNESCO General History of Africa. 8 vols. Berkeley: University of California Press, 1980–93.

Webster, J. B., and A. A. Boahen, with M. Tidy. *The Revolutionary Years: West Africa Since 1800*. New ed. London: Longman, 1980.

GLOSSARY

Aja
language spoken by the Fon and other West African peoples living between the Mono and Oueme rivers; also known as Ewe and Gbe

Amazon
popular European term for a female warrior in the Dahomean army

Annual Customs
a yearly celebration held in Dahomey at which the king received tax payments from his subjects and also dispensed gifts

appliqué
a cutout decoration fastened to a larger piece of material; technique used by Dahomean artists when creating cloth and umbrellas

calabash
a vessel made from the shell of a gourd and used throughout Africa to hold food and water

clan
a social group made up of people who trace their descent to a common ancestor

colonialism
political system under which a nation controls a foreign territory or people

cowries
small white shells used as currency in Dahomey and other African kingdoms

dokpwe
a cooperative work group formed by Dahomean villagers

dokpwegan
the village official who supervises the dokpwe and also presides at important community events such as funerals

dynasty
a powerful group or family that maintains its position over a period of time, as in the control of a kingdom for several generations

Fon	the major ethnic group of the kingdom of Dahomey
guild	an association of craftspeople or merchants
mercenary	a soldier who hires out his services to a foreign government
meu	the second-ranking official in the government of Dahomey; acted as the king's spokesman and had the power, along with the *migan*, to choose the heir to the throne
migan	the highest-ranking official in the government of Dahomey; functioned as the king's executioner and held authority over all Dahomeans who were not members of the royal family
musket	a firearm in use from the 16th through the 19th centuries
palm oil	oil extracted from the nuts of African palm trees; a major African export since the 19th century
Slave Coast	the region of West Africa between the mouth of the Volta River and the Lagos Channel; a major slave-exporting area between the 17th and 19th centuries
transatlantic slave trade	the traffic in human beings that exported millions of Africans to the Americas between 1500 and 1900
tribute	a payment by one ruler or nation to another as a token of submission or a guarantee of protection
vodun	one of the many gods making up the Dahomean religious system
ward	a division of a city created for political or administrative purposes

INDEX

Archaeologists have discovered many tools and art objects under Afghanistan's dry soil. These objects provide clues about what life was like in the region thousands of years ago.

anywhere in the world to make stone tools, cultivate crops, and raise livestock for food. Scientists have uncovered tools dating to 30,000 BCE in a rock shelter called Kara Kamar. In a cave near the city of Balkh, not far from Mazar-e Sharif, they found a collection of finely crafted stone and flint axes and scrapers dating back twenty thousand years. They also found a small limestone carving of a human face, one of the oldest images of a human ever unearthed.

The Aryan Conquest

In 1,500 BCE, a group of central Asian tribes, called the Aryans, were the first to cross over the Oxus River to invade what is now Afghanistan. The Aryans found the Afghan people living in small villages, raising livestock and growing crops. They also discovered that Afghans had built small cities, started governments, and established trading networks.

O VER THE COURSE OF THOUSANDS OF YEARS, THE land that is now Afghanistan has been both blessed and cursed. It is positioned between the sites of major ancient civilizations in Europe, East Asia, India, Arabia, and Persia. Trade routes between kingdoms and empires crisscrossed the land. As travelers and traders passed through Afghanistan, they shared their cultures and customs, and turned many parts of Afghanistan into a treasure trove of diverse art, architecture, music, poetry, philosophy, language, and religion.

Afghanistan gained much from being near rich and powerful civilizations, but it also suffered nonstop invasions and battles. As the armies of the warring empires advanced on each other, Afghanistan lay trapped in the middle.

Opposite: **Traders have been crisscrossing the land that is now Afghanistan for thousands of years, bringing goods from East Asia to Europe and Africa.**

Ancient Times

More than two million years ago, ancestors of modern humans lived in caves and rock shelters, and along river valleys in what is now Afghanistan. Many archaeologists believe that early humans in Afghanistan were some of the first people

The Aryans had come to conquer, and conquer they did, killing thousands. The Aryans named the region Ariana and ruled for more than a thousand years. During Aryan rule, the prophet Zoroaster lived and preached in Balkh, which was the capital of an empire called Bactria. The city blossomed into a great cultural center.

Macedonians and Mauryans

In 540 BCE, Cyrus the Great, the leader of a Persian dynasty based in what is now Iran, invaded Ariana. For the next two hundred years, nearly all of what is present-day Afghanistan was under Persian rule. But in 330 BCE, a young Macedonian

Cyrus the Great conquered lands throughout southwestern and central Asia. He allowed the peoples he conquered to maintain their traditions and practice their own religions.

Alexander the Great was a brilliant military leader. He created an empire that reached from the Mediterranean Sea to the Himalayas.

prince from Greece, known as Alexander the Great, began dismantling the Persian dynasty. By 328 BCE, his armies had taken control of Herat and Kandahar. As they pressed northeast into Bactria, Alexander's soldiers were overcome by the cold, snow, and harsh terrain. The Bactrian villagers were terrified of these strangers. They brought them food and their belongings and begged that their lives be spared. Eventually, Alexander succeeded in overtaking Bactria and the areas around Kabul and Jalalabad.

Alexander the Great died a young man, leaving no heir. Without a clear leader, his Macedonian Empire began to unravel. Meanwhile, India was becoming more powerful under the Mauryan dynasty, while southern Afghanistan was growing more unruly. To make peace with the Mauryan

Afghanistan

Contents

Cover photo:
Young Afghan
woman

Picking crocus flowers

Markhor

"Afghans to the Top"

ON JULY 19, 2009, TWO MEN—ONE A FARMER AND THE other a cook—became the first Afghan citizens to scale Afghanistan's highest mountain. Wanting to become part of the history of their ancient land, the men proudly staked the red, green, and black flag of their country atop Mount Noshaq, a peak towering 24,557 feet (7,485 meters) in the Hindu Kush mountain range. Malang Daria and Amruddin Sanjar began their journey from a small, isolated village walled in by massive, snow-covered mountains. Their trek was a challenge almost beyond measure: there were no trails to follow, and there was not much shelter from the icy rocks and swirling winds.

Afghans are familiar with rugged, steep terrain, yet not many choose to scale any of Afghanistan's many extraordinary peaks. Mountain climbing requires time and money, and few Afghans have the free time or the money to pursue such a challenge. But Daria and Sanjar decided to do it. They focused on their goal and trained intensely. Sanjar says that he has the "temper of a pirate." Daria is equally courageous.

Opposite: **The Hindu Kush is a western extension of the Himalayas, the highest mountains on Earth.**

Malang Daria was one of two Afghans who climbed Mount Noshaq in 2009.

Fortunately, their determination did not go unnoticed. A group of French people working in Afghanistan helped finance their efforts. They called the expedition "Afghans to the Top." Said one of the French supporters, "It is a symbolic

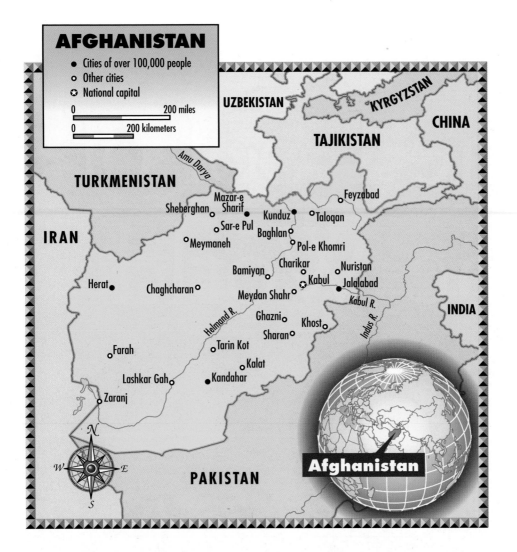

expedition, to plant an Afghan flag as a symbol of hope and achievement for Afghanistan." The country has faced many decades of war and strife, the supporter noted. The triumph of Daria and Sanjar showed the ability of Afghans "to overcome the difficulties and bring peace and success to a country torn apart by thirty years of war."

The Roof of the World

AFGHANISTAN HAS ONE OF THE MOST DRAMATIC landscapes on Earth. From barren deserts to craggy rock outcroppings to massive mountains, the land is not for the timid. More than half of Afghanistan is higher than 1 mile (1.6 kilometers) above sea level. That is why the nation is sometimes called the Roof of the World. The climate can be harsh. Afghanistan suffers searing temperatures in summer and below-freezing chills in winter, as well as sandstorms, earthquakes, and droughts.

Opposite: **Snow-covered peaks rise above Bamiyan Valley, west of Kabul.**

The Lay of the Land

Over the years, Afghanistan has been a crossroads connecting Iran, India, and China. It lies in central Asia, with Iran to the west, and Pakistan to the south and east. To the north, Afghanistan shares borders with Turkmenistan, Uzbekistan, Tajikistan, and China. In area, it measures 251,825 square miles (652,225 square kilometers), roughly the size of the country of France or the U.S. state of Texas.

Afghanistan's Geographic Features

Area: 251,825 square miles (652,225 sq km)

Highest Elevation: Mount Noshaq, 24,557 feet (7,485 m) above sea level

Lowest Elevation: Amu Darya riverbed, 846 feet (258 m) above sea level

Widest Point East to West: About 770 miles (1,240 km)

Widest Point North to South: About 350 miles (560 km)

Longest River Entirely within Afghanistan: Helmand River, about 715 miles (1,150 km)

Longest Navigable River: Amu Darya, about 1,600 miles (2,575 m)

Highest Recorded Temperature: 122°F (50°C) in Farah in August 2009

Lowest Recorded Temperature: −62°F (−52°C) in Shahrak in January 1964

Average Annual Precipitation: 12 inches (30 cm)

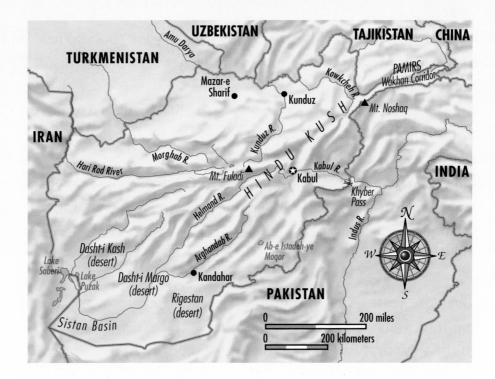

Afghanistan has three geographic regions. The northern plains feature rolling hills and grasslands, river valleys, a lake region, and pastureland. The Hindu Kush, a chain of the Himalaya mountain range, cuts across the middle of Afghanistan. These huge mountains and the high desert around them form the central highlands. The rugged terrain of the south includes desert, barren cliffs, and cave-filled hills. Several rivers, including the Helmand River—the longest to flow entirely within Afghanistan—rise in the central mountains and flow across the arid southern plateau.

An Afghan leads a camel train through the mountains. People have been using camels in the region for more than two thousand years.

Hardy sheep graze on Afghanistan's dry plains.

The Northern Plains

Many people around the world are struck by the beauty of the snowcapped Himalayas. Most Afghans, however, prefer green valleys and flowing rivers, like those in northeastern Afghanistan. This region is home to most of the country's farmland. Shepherds raise goats and sheep in the valleys and on the grassy plains. Although little rain falls—an average of less than 17 inches (43 centimeters) a year—many rivers flow down from the mountains and provide water for crops and pasturelands. The largest of these rivers is the Amu Darya, known as the Oxus River in ancient times. The Amu Darya

A Look at Afghanistan's Cities

Kabul, the capital of Afghanistan, is the nation's largest city, with nearly two million residents. Kandahar, in southern Afghanistan, is the country's second-largest city, with a population of about 470,000. Since ancient times, Kandahar has been the area's main trading center. Alexander the Great, the son of a Macedonian king, founded the city in the fourth century BCE, recognizing its ideal location along trade routes.

With nearly 400,000 residents, Herat (right), in western Afghanistan, is the nation's third-largest city. More than five centuries ago, Queen Gawhar Shad convinced her husband to move the seat of their empire

to Herat. The queen encouraged artists, architects, craftspeople, poets, and musicians to move to the city. She commissioned shrines and public buildings built in the Islamic style of architecture, with elaborate blue-tiled domes. Today, Herat, with its comfortable climate and cultural legacy, continues to be a center for arts and commerce.

Mazar-e Sharif, Afghanistan's fast-growing and fourth-largest city, is home to about 375,000 people, mostly ethnic Tajiks. The city is home to the Shrine of Hazrat Ali, also known as the Blue Mosque (left). The building is renowned for its incredible decoration.

separates Afghanistan from its northern neighbors. Farmers rely on the Amu Darya to water their fields. They channel the water into ditches and tunnels called *qarats*. In recent years, the amount of irrigation has decreased the flow of the Amu Darya, and the river no longer reaches the Aral Sea as it once did. Instead, it dries up before it gets there.

The Central Highlands

The central highlands occupy most of the land in Afghanistan. The region's greatest feature is the towering Hindu Kush mountains. The Siah Kuh, Turkistan, Malmand, and Pamir mountain chains also crisscross the region. The Hindu Kush is a remarkable uprising of the earth, with narrow, slightly forested valleys climbing steeply toward peaks that reach an average of 23,000 feet (7,000 m). Glaciers and snow cover the

Few people live in the dry, rugged Pamir Mountains.

mountaintops, and when they melt, they become the sources of most of the country's rivers. Five main rivers flow north from the mountains to form the Amu Darya. Other rivers flow south from the Hindu Kush, cutting through the barren deserts before drying up.

The Wakhan Corridor in the northeast portion of the central highlands is a remote finger of land that extends 220 miles (354 km) toward China. In the easternmost part, the Hindu Kush and the Pamir Mountains surround high, broad valleys carved by the Wakhan and Pamir Rivers. It is a wild and windswept place, where ethnic Wakhi and Kyrgyz people grow wheat and barley and herd sheep, goats, and yaks. At the western end of the Wakhan Corridor, the Pamir and Wakhan Rivers join to form the Panj River, whose roaring rapids slice through the Hindu Kush and create sharp, craggy mountain walls and narrow, forbidding valleys.

Animals graze in a valley in the Wakhan Corridor. This region was not part of Afghanistan until 1894, when Great Britain and Russia drew new borders to separate their empires.

Moving Land

Earth's outer layer is broken up into several huge pieces called tectonic plates, which fit together like a jigsaw puzzle. Earthquakes are more common along the borders between two plates. The Hindu Kush and the Pamirs lie along the border between the Indian and the Eurasian tectonic plates. These plates cause major earthquakes as they smash into each other, moving at a record-breaking 1.7 inches (4.3 cm) per year. Each year, several significant earthquakes shake the region.

Nuristan, a province south of the Wakhan Corridor in the Hindu Kush, is almost entirely mountainous, imprisoned by steep, forested walls of rock. Only 1 percent of the land is flat. It is extremely difficult to get around in this area—most travel can only be done on foot. Buried in the mountainsides are gemstones such as sapphires, quartzes, topazes, and aquamarines.

In the eastern portion of the central highlands is a high basin with a somewhat temperate climate. Average tempera-

Through the Mountains

High mountain passes (called *kotals*) are crucial to travel in Afghanistan. Conquerors, explorers, and traders have cut through the Afghan mountains along passes that are still in use today.

Kotal	Elevation	
Khyber	3,369 feet (1,027 m)	Afghanistan-Pakistan border crossing
Salang	12,723 feet (3,878 m)	Connects Kabul to the north and south
Shabar	10,695 feet (3,260 m)	Connects Kabul to the north
Wakhjir	16,152 feet (4,923 m)	Connects Wakhan Corridor to China

The Bamiyan Valley is one of the most fertile parts of Afghanistan.

tures in this region, around the cities of Kabul and Jalalabad, are 77 degrees Fahrenheit (25 degrees Celsius) in July, and about 32°F (0°C) in January. From its source in the Hindu Kush, the Kabul River flows past Kabul and Jalalabad toward Pakistan. The river is used heavily for irrigation, and the wide valleys support a variety of agricultural crops. Hard rains sometimes fall on Jalalabad and the surrounding areas in spring, causing flooding.

In the Bamiyan Valley, located west of Kabul in the central highlands, the land flattens into high, broad plains that are surrounded by the snowcapped Koh-i-Baba and Hindu Kush mountains. The valley features rock cliffs, green fields, wetlands, and lakes. Among the valley's sandstone cliffs is a

The End of the Buddhas

Although many people appreciate the Bamiyan Valley for its striking landscape, it is best known now for what no longer exists. The valley is ringed by dramatic sandstone cliffs. From the fifth through the seventh centuries, Chinese Buddhists explored the area and built altars into the cliffs. They carved massive statues of the Buddha in the cliffs and made details out of mud, straw, paint, and plaster. One Buddha stood 175 feet (53 m) tall and another 125 feet (38 m) tall. The statues could be seen from anywhere in the city of Bamiyan. But one day in 2001, soldiers in the Taliban army, who believed the statues were idols that might be worshipped by non-Muslims, blew them up. People around the world mourned the destruction of these ancient treasures.

startling rock formation known as the Bamiyan Dragon. The dragon is a ridge of lava nearly 1,000 feet (300 m) long that was split open by an earthquake. Water from springs deep below the surface surges upward with a grumbling, moaning sound. Beyond the dragon lies the Band-e Amir lake region. The lakes are the craters of old volcanoes. Because of mineral deposits, they have an astonishing deep blue-black color.

Near the border of Iran—far from any large body of water— the western portion of the central highlands unfolds into a region of remote mountains and dry grasslands called the steppe. Powerful winds howl across the steppe. No trees grow there, so there is nothing to block the path of the winds. Year-round temperatures average 60°F (15°C), and precipitation, falling mostly as snow, averages about 10 inches (25 cm) a year.

The South

The southern region of Afghanistan is chiefly desert and dry, treeless mountains. In the southeast is the large Rigestan Desert. Two smaller deserts lie north of the Helmand River. The river provides water to irrigate the nearby valleys.

Summer temperatures in the south are brutally hot. Powerful winds blow dust and sand everywhere. Though the area is very dry, heavy spring storms rage up from the Arabian Sea and pelt the eastern area with up to 40 inches (100 cm) of rain. In the southwest, winds are fierce during the summer months, blowing sand into rapidly shifting dunes. Hot dust storms swirl across the southern desert at speeds of up to 110 miles per hour (175 kilometers per hour).

Natural Disasters

Afghans have faced more than their share of natural disasters. Earthquakes frequently rattle northern areas and sometimes send deadly landslides down mountains. At higher elevations, avalanches are common hazards. In spring, melting snows cause flash floods and mudslides that cover villages. In the south and east, droughts lasting years can occur, destroying crops and other vegetation.

The Natural World

24

ALTHOUGH AFGHANISTAN IS MOSTLY DRY AND mountainous, it has an amazing variety of plants and animals that are native to Europe, eastern Asia, and India. The Hindu Kush separates animals and plants native to India from those to the north and west.

Mammals and Birds

A wide array of wildlife lives in the grasslands, deserts, marshes, forests, and mountain ranges of Afghanistan. The nation is home to nine species of wild cats—as many as are found in the jungles of Africa—including the lynx, the cheetah, Pallas's cat, and the endangered snow leopard. In northern Afghanistan are wolves, wild boar, black bears, brown bears, jackals, striped hyenas, monkeys, three species of mountain goat, yaks, and wild sheep. One species is the Marco Polo sheep, which have giant horns.

Animals living on the steppes and in the deserts include wild donkeys; antelopes such as oryx and gazelles; and

Marco Polo Sheep

First described to the Western world by the Italian adventurer Marco Polo in 1273, the Marco Polo sheep lives only in the Pamir Mountains. The largest species of wild sheep in the world, these animals weigh as much as 300 pounds (140 kilograms), and their huge horns often measure 6 feet (2 m) long. Marco Polo sheep range across wide-open spaces, and when confronted by humans or other animals, they do not run away or hide. Marco Polo noted that the people living in the mountains hunted the sheep. They ate the meat and made bowls, tools, and fence posts from the horns. Today, some hunters still prize the Marco Polo sheep, causing the animal to become endangered.

smaller mammals such as hares, bats, hedgehogs, shrews, and mongooses. More than 450 species of birds are found in Afghanistan, including songbirds, buzzards, raptors, ducks, partridges, flamingos, and the rare Siberian crane.

Rare Bird

Until recently, the world's rarest bird, the large-billed reed warbler, had not been seen since 1867. Then, in 2010, a flock of the birds were discovered in the remote Wakhan Corridor. The director of the Afghan National Environmental Protection Agency was thrilled. Not only was the bird not extinct, but many of them lived in Afghanistan. The agency immediately placed the bird on its protected species list.

Reptiles and Insects

Afghanistan is home to many reptiles, scorpions, and insects. One of the most deadly snakes in the country is the saw-scaled viper. It lives in hot sandy soils, scrublands, dry forests, and near riverbanks. It can climb into trees to rest or to hunt. The snake is nervous and quick to strike. When disturbed, it wraps itself in a double coil and rubs its sides together, making a loud, scratchy sound. There is no cure for a saw-scaled viper's venom. When the snake bites, the victim often dies.

Another deadly snake, the Oxus cobra, lives in rocky hills, caves, and tree hollows. It is not aggressive, but when it feels threatened, it lifts its upper body and spreads its hood wide. When the Oxus cobra bites, it chews viciously, and its venom chokes off the airways of its victim.

The saw-scaled viper is among the world's deadliest snakes. Its bite kills thousands of people every year.

The Darkened Sky

Every few years, the northern plains of Afghanistan are overcome by swarms of locusts. These horned grasshoppers fill the sky so that it looks black. When they land, the ground appears to be moving. The locusts eat every morsel they find in the fields. The last major locust outbreak was in 2008, and residents of one farming community north of Herat killed more than 300 tons (270 metric tons) of locusts in just a few weeks.

From Wild to Tame

How does a wild animal become tame enough to keep? How does a field of wild grass become a field of wheat? The food grown today and the world's pets and livestock were once wild species. Humans selected young wild animals they thought

People in central Asia domesticated goats between eight and nine thousand years ago.

would be good for milk, eggs, or meat, or that would be useful as work animals. They bred them so that the qualities they most preferred would be emphasized. Likewise, humans chose plants that would be the most nourishing and that would grow well in their region.

The people in what is now Afghanistan developed a great many important species. Some of the animals whose ancestors ran wild in the region are today's farmyard goats, sheep, cows, horses, and mules. Some of the wild plants that early Afghans cultivated were wheat, barley, grapes, melons, dates, pistachios, almonds, and carrots.

Afghan Hound

The long-haired, noble Afghan hound is a dog originally bred by nomads in the mountains of Afghanistan more than four thousand years ago. The Afghan hound has large feet and strong hips, so that it can easily climb rock ridges, hop over boulders, and run quickly across open plains. Its teeth are large, which is useful for capturing and killing prey. Its coat is long for warmth. In many places in the world today, the Afghan hound is still used for hunting and herding. It is also often a clever and faithful pet.

Bactrian Camel

The two-humped, or Bactrian camel, is native to an area in northern Afghanistan that in ancient times was called Bactria. The Bactrian camel is no longer found in the wild in Afghanistan, but some Afghans use domesticated camels. The Bactrian camel is a remarkable creature. It can go without water for weeks at a time. When water is available, it can drink and store 15 gallons (60 liters) at a time. Bactrian camels can swim, run 40 miles per hour (65 kph), and carry loads up to 600 pounds (270 kg).

Plants

Thousands of kinds of plants grow in Afghanistan, including more than eight hundred species that are found nowhere else in the world. Pine trees grow in the high mountain areas of the Hindu Kush and the Wakhan Corridor. In the lower regions, oak, cedar, and maple trees are found. Along the river valleys, wild relatives of common fruit trees such as apple, almond, and pear grow. In the woodlands and on some of the slopes of the Hindu Kush are forests of almond and pistachio trees, which are native to Afghanistan.

In the east, pine, cedar, mulberries, and flowering rhododendrons thrive. Scruffy, thorny plants such as junipers are found in the high basin near Kabul and throughout the upper mountain woodlands. Grasses grow on the steppes. Among

Poppies grow wild in the Afghan grasslands.

the flowers that shoot up in spring near Herat are irises, poppies, tulips, and lilies. In the spring, much of the ground is green, but by summer nearly all of the plants have died.

Desert Plant

A plant called glasswort helps people survive in the Afghan desert. This low, bushy plant thrives in dry, sandy, salty soil. Its roots hold sand in place against raging windstorms. Its stalks and branches provide a nearly smokeless fuel for fires. Desert animals eat the glasswort, and it is sometimes used to fertilize crops. Glasswort can even be ground into a flour that is used in making flat bread.

Markhors have dramatic spiraling horns. The horns on male markhors can grow more than 60 inches (150 cm) long.

Conservation

Afghanistan passed its first environmental law in 2005. The National Environmental Protection Agency was also established in that year. The agency quickly went to work to determine which plants and animals in Afghanistan were being overharvested or were in danger of becoming extinct.

The agency has set up four national parks, one national reserve, two wildlife reserves, four waterfowl sanctuaries, and other protected areas. The Band-e Amir lakes region was Afghanistan's first national park, established in 2009. It includes six lakes and 228 square miles (590 sq km) of public land.

Protected animals in Afghanistan include the markhor, a wild goat whose horns are highly desired for use in herbal medicine. The snow leopard is also protected. This animal is

prized for its fur and despised for attacking goats and sheep. Herders throughout the Hindu Kush and the Pamirs will shoot a snow leopard on sight. A snow leopard pelt can sell for US$10,000 or more.

In Afghanistan, nearly 80 percent of the people rely on natural resources such as fish, ducks, wild game, and trees for survival. But in this dry and mountainous country, such resources are limited. A great many Afghans are poor. They fish and hunt game for food, and cut down trees for fuel and for building materials. Replacing what has been taken requires time, money, education, and effort. It is difficult for people to give up their traditional way of life, yet the traditional way of life is taking its toll on the land.

The Band-e Amir lakes sit high in the Hindu Kush, about 10,000 feet (3,000 m) above sea level.

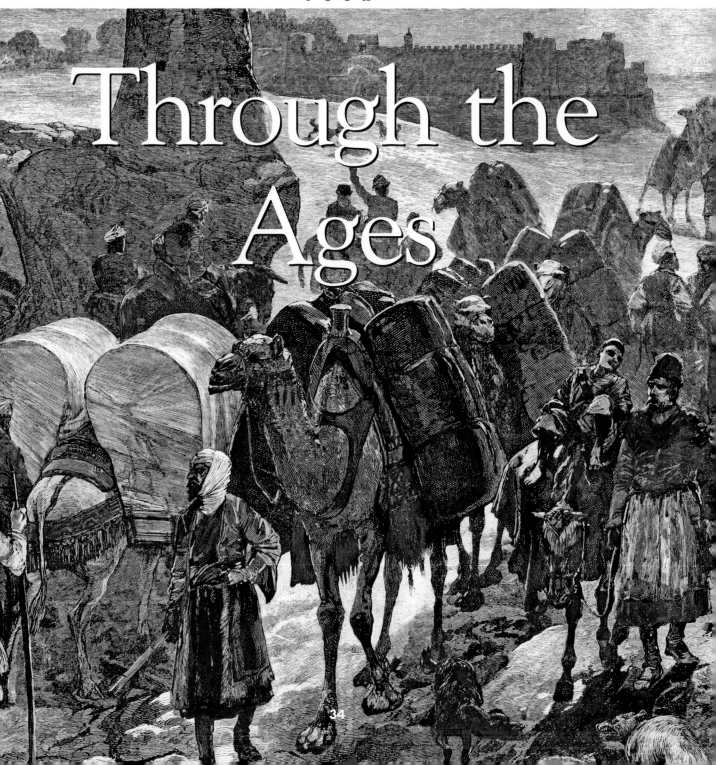

Through the Ages

Frontispiece: Man praying at a mosque in Kabul

Consultant: Thomas Gouttierre, Dean of International Studies and Programs and Director of the Center for Afghanistan Studies, University of Nebraska-Omaha

Please note: All statistics are as up-to-date as possible at the time of publication.

Book production by The Design Lab

Library of Congress Cataloging-in-Publication Data

Bjorklund, Ruth.
  Afghanistan/by Ruth Bjorklund.
    p. cm.—(Enchantment of the world. Second series)
  Includes bibliographical references and index.
  ISBN-13: 978-0-531-25350-2 (lib. bdg.)
  ISBN-10: 0-531-25350-3 (lib. bdg.)
  1. Afghanistan—Juvenile literature. I. Title. II. Series.
  DS351.5.B54 2012
  958.1—dc22   2011013627

Afghanistan

By Ruth Bjorklund

Enchantment of the World™
Second Series

Children's Press®
An Imprint of Scholastic Inc.

NEW YORK TORONTO LONDON AUCKLAND SYDNEY
MEXICO CITY NEW DELHI HONG KONG
DANBURY, CONNECTICUT

dynasty, Alexander's officers traded southeastern Afghanistan and the Kandahar region to India for a generous amount of gold and five hundred war elephants.

While Kandahar and the southeastern portion of Afghanistan were under Mauryan rule, most of the rest of Afghanistan remained under Macedonian rule. The climate in Bactria was similar to the climate in Greece. Being more than a year's march from home, the Macedonians attempted to re-create the culture of Greece in Bactria. They grew papyrus for papermaking, and ate typical Mediterranean foods, such as olive oil and goat. In 1963, scientists studying the Bactrian region uncovered a Greek palace, marketplaces, theaters, and temples honoring Greek gods.

Eventually, the Macedonian Empire fell apart. By 300 BCE, much of Afghanistan had come under the rule of Ashoka, the

Bactria has a rich artistic history. These stone Bactrian figures are about four thousand years old.

Indian king of the Mauryan dynasty. Ashoka was often brutal, slaughtering anyone who insulted or resisted him. But in 250 BCE, Ashoka had a change of heart. He felt guilty for all the suffering he had caused and turned to the Buddhist religion for comfort. Throughout his empire, including Afghanistan, Ashoka spread his Buddhist beliefs. He sent out missionaries and built thousands of Buddhist monasteries, shrines, and stupas (dome-shaped Buddhist monuments). The rest of his reign passed in peace.

The Kushans Take Control

Peace did not last long, however. After Ashoka's death, the Mauryan dynasty ended. At the same time, groups in China were uniting under the rule of a single tribe, the Chin. As the Chin dynasty became more powerful, they pushed out other

Ashoka's name means "painless" or "without sorrow."

The Silk Road

About two thousand years ago, Europeans began trading for some of the luxuries produced by civilizations in the East. From China, they desired silk, a fabric both beautiful and durable. Europeans also prized spices, perfumes, gems, beads, and muslin cloth from India. From Southeast Asia and the East Indies, they sought cinnamon, nutmeg, cloves, and incense. From Persia, they traded for glass and carpets.

European rulers sent adventurers to the East to trade for goods and bring them back to their kingdoms. The traders brought wool, horses, jade, and wine to the East. They also brought goods from Africa, including ivory, gold, and ostriches for their feathers. Of particular interest to the Chinese was colored glass from the Mediterranean.

The traders traveled in groups, called caravans. They rode the eastern portion of the journey on Bactrian camels. The traders endured travel over incredibly rough terrain, and none were able to do the entire journey. Instead, they carried the cargo in relays. At the relay points, the traders stopped to exchange goods and barter for food and other necessities. All along the Silk Road, lively marketplaces and cities developed.

The Silk Road was not an actual road, but rather a series of trails. The trails eventually joined together in the area ruled by the Kushans in the Bactrian region of Afghanistan. The Kushans in Balkh were exceptionally skilled bargainers. Living amid Greek Macedonians, they had learned the Greek alphabet and language and were able to communicate with the Europeans. They made gold coins with royal faces and Greek writing, which was familiar to the Europeans. As a result, Balkh became an important stopping place and one of the wealthiest market cities along the Silk Road.

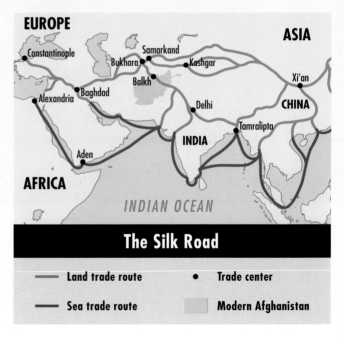

The Silk Road

Land trade route • Trade center

Sea trade route   Modern Afghanistan

The Kushans made Buddhism the official religion of their empire. Ruins of some Buddhist temples built by the Kushans still stand in Afghanistan.

Chinese tribes. Those tribes migrated toward Bactria, and around 150 BCE, five of the tribes joined forces to create the Kushan Empire. The Kushans took over Bactria and continued their march. They eventually controlled lands from the Aral Sea to India and to Persia. Though the Kushans brought war once again to Afghanistan, their empire set the stage for the creation of the Silk Road, an overland trade route between China, India, Persia, Arabia, and Europe.

The Kushan Empire ruled for three centuries before it was taken over by the Persian Sassanian Empire in 241 CE. The Sassanians practiced the Hindu religion and built many temples around Afghanistan. But early in the fifth century, war came again.

The White Hun Invasion

A group called the Hephthalites, or White Huns, had come to power. They gathered their armies near the Aral Sea and marched south and west, overrunning Bactria. In less than a hundred years, the White Huns took over all of Afghanistan. They destroyed temples, monasteries, public buildings, and great works of art. They slaughtered princes and soldiers, villagers, artists, musicians, teachers, and holy men. It took two centuries before the combined forces of the Persian armies and the Turkomans in central Asia were able to oust the White Huns. By this time, Afghanistan's great civilization lay in ruins.

Several different peoples active in the fifth century were called Huns. While the White Huns invaded Afghanistan, the Western Huns, led by Attila (above), invaded Europe.

The ruler Mahmud was a great supporter of artists, and Ghazni became a cultural capital. This painting from 1249 shows poets at his court.

The Rise of Islam

The seventh century brought about religious stirrings that would change the world. In Arabia, a prophet named Muhammad preached a new religion called Islam. A shared belief in the teachings of Muhammad united many Arabian kingdoms, and in 633, a year after Muhammad died, Arab armies defeated the Persians.

In 642, an Arab general ordered the armies to spread their empire across Afghanistan. At first, Afghans resisted, but eventually Balkh and Herat were overtaken. By the early eighth century, most of Afghanistan was under Muslim rule. The greatest Muslim ruler of the time was an Afghan named Mahmud of Ghazni. Mahmud established his empire in 998 and made its capital Ghazni, a city south of Kabul. As Mahmud's empire grew, Hindus and Buddhists were converted to Islam, and Ghazni became the center of Islamic power in the region. When Mahmud died, his empire weakened. In the early twelfth century, a Persian leader from Herat named Jahan-Suz, or "world burner," leveled the city of Ghazni.

The Mongol Invasion

As Ghazni burned, a tribe of forty thousand families north of the Gobi desert in China were forming an army. The people were called Mongols. The Mongols were livestock herders, skilled horsemen, and wildly fierce. In 1175, the chief, or khan, died, and his thirteen-year-old son became khan. At first, the Mongol armies had little faith in the boy's leadership.

Genghis Khan created the biggest empire the world has ever known. It spread over almost all of Asia and into Europe.

Mongol leader Timur encouraged trade, supported artists, and built schools.

But before long, the boy, whom they named Genghis Khan ("the very mighty chief"), had become a fearless warrior.

Genghis Khan set out to conquer the world. He and his army invaded Afghanistan in 1219. They destroyed the beautiful cities of Herat, Bamiyan, and Balkh. The Mongols leveled buildings, salted farmers' fields so nothing would grow, and damaged irrigation systems so crops could not be watered. Much of the land never recovered and is desert to this day.

After Genghis Khan, other conquerors plagued Afghanistan. One such man was the Mongol leader, Timur (sometimes called Tamerlane), who established his empire in 1370. At first, Timur sought destruction, but as his empire grew larger and wealthier, he tried to restore cities to their former glory. His son rebuilt Herat, and artists and traders returned. The Silk Road was revived.

Babur's Story

An Afghan prince named Babur, a great-great-great-grandson of Timur, wrote the first autobiography in the Islamic world. Born in 1483, Babur grew up in a beautiful, fertile valley in what is now Uzbekistan. When he was orphaned at age twelve, he inherited his father's small kingdom, but then he lost it. To regain what had been lost, he went into the forest to build an army and develop a plan. After three years, Babur led his army over the Hindu Kush into Kabul. He captured the city in 1504. He loved Kabul and built a home there. As he was fond of nature, his home was surrounded by a large garden filled with flowers, sculptures, and fountains.

Babur eventually left Kabul and took control of Kandahar, another important trading center. Then he marched on to India, where he based his kingdom, called the Moghul Empire.

Babur was an educated man, a devout follower of Islam, and a supporter of Persian arts and culture.

His autobiography, called the *Babur-nameh*, tells of his conquests and empire. But it also gives the world the first description of everyday life in Afghanistan, as well as the first description of Afghan geography, plants, animals, arts, architecture, music, and literature. Long after his death, his body was returned to Kabul and laid to rest in his garden, where an inscription reads, "If there is a paradise on earth, it is this, it is this, it is this!"

Becoming Afghanistan

For three centuries beginning in the 1400s, Afghanistan was under the influence of two empires, the Moghul of India and the Safavid of Persia. In 1722, Afghans revolted and conquered the Safavid Empire. In 1736, Nadir Shah, an Afghan chief, became king of Persia. He took over Kandahar and Herat, and marched toward India to attack the Moghuls. In 1747, he was killed. His successor, Ahmad Khan Abdali Durrani, changed the course of Afghan history.

The Crown Jewel

After Nadir Shah conquered the Moghul Empire, he held a victory celebration. During the celebration, he tricked the Moghul emperor into giving him his turban. Nadir Shah had been secretly told that the emperor hid his most prized and historic diamond in his turban. Some said the diamond had been stolen from the Hindu god Krishna.

When Nadir Shah unwrapped the turban, he was startled by the gem's beauty and called out "*Koh-i-noor*!" meaning "mountain of light." After Nadir Shah's death, Ahmad Khan Abdali Durrani kept the diamond with him in Kabul and declared it a symbol of his power. In 1849, after a century of conflict, the

Koh-i-noor diamond fell into the hands of the British. It was placed in the crown of Queen Victoria. Since then, both India and Afghanistan have claimed the diamond and want it returned. Today, the Koh-i-noor diamond is the largest gem in the British crown jewels.

ASIA

Kabul

ASIA

Arabian Sea

Bay of Bengal

AFRICA

Afghanistan, 1500–1800

▇ Moghul Empire, 1701	— Durrani dynasty, 1772
▇ Safavid Empire, 1722	— Modern Afghanistan

Ahmad Khan Durrani was a powerful general and a more just leader than Afghanistan had ever had. He set up a *loya jirga*, a grand council of tribal chiefs, and gave the chiefs authority to rule their own tribes. His method of ruling with a council of tribal chiefs would be a model for many future Afghan governments.

At first, his kingdom included only the traditional Pashtun region in southern Afghanistan. Eventually, he became the shah, or leader, of all Afghanistan and became known as

Ahmad Shah Durrani. He took over lands in parts of Moghul India, and by the end of the eighteenth century, Afghanistan was the most powerful Muslim empire in the world. Today, Ahmad Shah Durrani is known as the Father of Afghanistan.

In 1772, Ahmad Shah died, leaving behind twenty-three sons. None of them could govern as their father had. They fought among themselves in countless civil wars. By 1818, they had lost much of their former land. Civil wars and foreign attacks continued to wreak havoc on Afghanistan's land and government. In 1826, a new ruler, Dost Mohammad Khan, took over in Kabul. He was appointed emir, or prince, and was called Commander of the Faithful. He set out to regain former Afghan territory, but did not succeed.

Dost Mohammad Khan came to power in 1826. He ruled until 1863.

In the nineteenth century, Great Britain and Russia were the two most powerful nations in Europe. Great Britain had colonized India, and Russia had taken over much of central Asia. Each wanted to control Afghanistan to protect its territory and extend its empire. As the two countries fought each other, Afghanistan was caught in the middle of a decades-long conflict called the Great Game.

Dost Mohammad wanted to use Britain and Russia to his own advantage. He asked the British for military help, and when they refused, he asked Russia. This angered the British, and in 1839 they invaded Afghanistan, beginning the first Anglo-Afghan War. Afghans in Kabul rebelled, and in four days, the British had lost three-quarters of their invading army. The British returned later and destroyed Kabul's marketplace.

In 1863, Dost Mohammad's son Sher Ali Khan took over the throne. It was difficult for him to keep Russia and Britain from taking over his country. Then, in 1878, he did a favor for the Russians, and the British once again declared war on Afghanistan. During this conflict, the Second Anglo-Afghan War, the British occupied Kandahar and Kabul, and installed Abdur Rahman, a grandson of Dost Mohammad, as king. The British allowed Abdur Rahman to rule inside Afghanistan, but they kept control of Afghanistan's foreign relations.

Abdur Rahman tried to strengthen the central Afghan government. He encouraged foreign scientists and doctors to come to Kabul and help modernize the country. His son, Habibullah Khan, followed in his footsteps, modernizing

The British captured Ghazni during the Second Anglo-Afghan War.

Afghanistan and staying on the good side of the British. He established schools and brought Western medicine to Afghan hospitals. During his reign, both electricity and the automobile came to Afghanistan.

The trouble with the British had not completely ended, however. Habibullah governed Afghanistan through World War I (1914–1918), but during the war years, he avoided siding with Britain. The Turks, to whom the Afghans had closer ties, fought with Britain's enemies: Austria, Hungary, and Germany. Many Afghans wanted Habibullah Khan to enter the war and fight against the British. Habibullah declined and was eventually assassinated.

When his son, Emir Amanullah, came to power, he wasted no time in declaring Afghanistan's independence. He invaded British India, beginning the Third Anglo-Afghan War. The

In 1919, a group of Afghan delegates signed the peace treaty that ended the Third Anglo-Afghan War.

British were worn out after four years of war and fought weakly. In 1919, they signed a peace treaty, establishing borders and giving Afghanistan full control of its foreign affairs. It was the first time in nearly two thousand years that Afghanistan was free from the rule of any foreign power.

Modernizing Afghanistan

In 1917, communists in Russia took control of the Russian government. They believed that property should be owned in common and that the government should run the economy. Soon, Russia banded together with other central Asian countries to become the Union of Soviet Socialist Republics, or USSR. The Soviets were eager to stay friendly with the Afghans. But most Afghans were anticommunist, and Amanullah did not trust the Soviets any more than he did the British.

Still, in May 1921, the two nations signed a treaty. The Soviets supplied Afghanistan with money, technology, and military assistance. With the Soviet support, Amanullah became very powerful and changed his title from emir to king. He changed the Afghan government, proposing new laws to replace tribal laws and setting up a new form of legislature. He adopted the nation's first constitution in 1923 and established a new unit of currency, the afghani.

Amanullah also established diplomatic ties with European and Asian countries, and through his travels, brought home a flurry of new ideas. Some of the modern reforms he suggested, especially those giving more rights to women, angered traditional tribal chiefs. In 1929, a civil war erupted over whether the country should adopt modern ideas or stay with traditional customs. Amanullah fled

During his years in power, Amanullah Khan worked to modernize Afghanistan.

to Europe, where he died in 1960. The new Afghan leaders created a constitution that included changes to modernize the country, but the changes were not as far-reaching as Amanullah's.

In November 1933, nineteen-year-old Muhammad Zahir Shah took the throne. He would be Afghanistan's last king. During the early years of his rule, he and his ministers improved education, encouraged the publication of newspapers, and built highways and railroads.

In 1953, he appointed his cousin Mohammad Daoud as prime minister. Daoud wanted to modernize Afghanistan and improve the economy. To fund his many projects, he sought aid from both the United States and the Soviet Union. In 1955, the Soviets offered Daoud a US$100 million loan and gave him US$25 million in other aid.

In 1964, King Zahir called for the loya jirga to meet. By winter, Afghanistan had a new constitution. The new law of the land called for a constitutional monarchy and a democratic legislature. The king would still rule, but his decisions had to be approved by a two-house legislature. The constitution also gave women the right to vote.

Divided Land

In 1947, India became independent from Great Britain. Most Indians were Hindus. Indian Muslims wanted their own independent nation, so Pakistan was created. The boundary between Pakistan and Afghanistan cut across traditional Pashtun lands. Families were divided, with some family members in Afghanistan and others in Pakistan. Many Pashtuns argued that they should have their own country, Pashtunistan.

Unfortunately, the new constitution did not end Afghan infighting. Daoud renewed his friendship with the Soviets, which angered Afghan Muslims because they did not want Soviet communists, who were not religious, having any power over them. When Daoud tried to satisfy the Muslims, communist Afghans rebelled. Daoud was assassinated in 1978.

Communists took over the Afghan government and strengthened ties with the Soviet Union. Conflict increased. Many Muslim leaders were imprisoned, and Muslims rebelled against the communist government. The situation was chaotic. If a civil war broke out, the Soviets would lose both a political ally and their financial investment in Afghanistan. In December 1979, Soviet troops invaded Afghanistan to end the rebellion.

Soviet tanks moved into Afghanistan in 1979. They stayed for ten years.

The mujahidin didn't have big weapons to use in their fight against the Soviets. But they knew the land well and could hide easily in the rugged mountains.

The Resistance

The Soviets underestimated the ability of the Afghan people to fight back. They also underestimated the importance of religion to Afghans. Tribal leaders who traditionally fought among themselves cast aside their differences and formed a resistance army. The fighters called themselves the mujahidin, or "holy warriors."

The Soviets and the Afghan army under their control numbered more than one hundred thousand well-armed troops. The mujahidin were mostly small bands of fighters. But they had the sympathy of much of the world. Pakistan,

China, and the United States condemned the Soviet invasion, and sent supplies and weapons to the mujahidin. Though outnumbered, the mujahidin were not outsmarted. They attacked quickly and then faded back into their hideouts in the mountains.

As combat continued, the Soviet people grew angry about the high cost of war and urged their leaders to put an end to the violence. The mujahidin refused to agree to a truce. In 1989, the Soviets withdrew their troops anyway.

The communist Afghan government continued to fight the mujahidin. A mujahidin leader named Ahmad Shah Massoud helped form the Northern Alliance, a group of soldiers who wanted to see the fall of the communist government. In 1992, after two million Afghans had died, and untold numbers of homes, cities, villages, farmland, and livestock had been lost, the Northern Alliance took over the government in Kabul.

The Rise of the Taliban

The Northern Alliance members soon began fighting among themselves. Ethnic Pashtuns, Tajiks, and Uzbeks in the government could not find common ground. The mujahidin returned to their villages and became aggressive toward people from other tribes. They set up roadblocks, captured food and supplies from other tribes, and demanded tolls from travelers. The government had little control. The time was ripe for another change.

In southeastern Afghanistan, a Muslim religious leader, or cleric, called Mullah Omar took a stand against the abuses of the mujahidin warlords. He believed in strict, traditional

Under Taliban rule, women had to cover their entire bodies, even their faces.

Islamic law, and he wanted to rein in the lawlessness he saw around him. Along the Pakistan border, Muslim clerics established schools, called madrassas, which were devoted to studying the holy book of Islam, the Qur'an. The students were called Taliban, meaning "religious student."

Mullah Omar (*mullah* means "teacher") started to form small bands of Taliban to help him control villages where the mujahidin warlords were mistreating people. Village by village, the Taliban soldiers started taking over local governments. At first, many people were grateful to feel a sense of order again.

In 1996, the Taliban seized Kabul and took over the national government. The governments of Saudi Arabia, the United Arab Emirates, and Pakistan recognized the Taliban as the official government of Afghanistan.

The Taliban established strict discipline and rules. Most girls could not attend school, and most women could not work. Because most Afghan teachers were women, many schools closed. Females were forced to wear a burqa, an ankle-length hooded garment that covers the head and face. Moreover, women were not to leave their homes any more than necessary. Men were to wear turbans and *shalwars*, or loose trousers, and they were not supposed to shave their beard. Many activities, sports, and children's games were banned, as were televisions and radios. Punishment for disobedience was brutal. Afghan villagers feared the Taliban. Many urban Afghans, whose religious beliefs were more liberal, fled the country.

The Cloak of the Prophet

In 1768, Ahmad Shah Durrani acquired the most treasured relics in all of Afghanistan: a cloak and a lock of hair said to have belonged to the Prophet Muhammad. The sacred items were put in a shrine in Kandahar. The cloak is only displayed in times of crisis; the last time it was shown amid a crisis was during a cholera epidemic in the 1930s. In 1994, Mullah Omar (left) wanted to claim the title "Amir-Al-Momineen" (commander of the faithful). Though he rarely came before the public, on this day he stood on the roof of the shrine before thousands of followers and held the Prophet's cloak aloft to symbolize his power.

Al-Qaeda, a terrorist group led by a man named Osama bin Laden, shared many of the Taliban's religious beliefs. Bin Laden came from a wealthy family in Saudi Arabia. He moved to southern Afghanistan to set up camps to train his soldiers, and he lived alongside the Taliban. The two groups supported one another, and bin Laden helped finance the Taliban's rise to power. His mission went beyond Afghanistan, however. He wanted to punish the Western world. On September, 9, 2001, two men posing as journalists interviewed the Northern Alliance leader Ahmad Shah Massoud, who led the opposi-

Osama bin Laden believed that the culture and policies of Western nations were harming Islam.

tion to the Taliban. The journalists were actually al-Qaeda suicide bombers. They had explosives strapped to their bodies. When they blew themselves up, they also killed Massoud. Two days later, al-Qaeda members flew jet airliners into the Twin Towers of the World Trade Center in New York City and the Pentagon building near Washington, D.C., and crashed another plane in Pennsylvania. In total, more than three thousand people were killed.

The United States responded by attacking Afghanistan. By November 2001, U.S. forces and the Northern Alliance had removed the Taliban from power. Bin Laden and al-Qaeda, as well as the Taliban, retreated to the mountains in southeastern Afghanistan. (U.S. forces finally killed bin Laden in 2011 in Pakistan.)

The man chosen to be president after the Taliban were defeated was a Pashtun politician named Hamid Karzai. Karzai strengthened the police force and developed programs to restore safe drinking water, electricity, farmland, and passable roadways. He traveled the world asking for money to help, returning home with more than US$5 billion. In October 2004, by popular vote, Karzai defeated twenty-two other candidates to become the first elected president of Afghanistan.

Over the next five years, the U.S. presence in the country grew, and so did the influence of the Taliban. Karzai was again elected president in 2009, although many objected to the voting process. Since then, surprise bombings in Herat, Kabul, and the north have shaken Afghans' sense of security. Peace and reconstruction will be a long time coming.

Governing Afghanistan

62

S INCE THE RULE OF CYRUS THE GREAT IN 550 BCE, more than forty flags have flown over Afghanistan. In the past one hundred years alone, Afghanistan's flag has changed at least ten times as the government has changed. Although Afghanistan is an ancient civilization, it is always remaking itself.

Opposite: **Hamid Karzai was elected president of Afghanistan in 2004. He was elected a second time in 2009.**

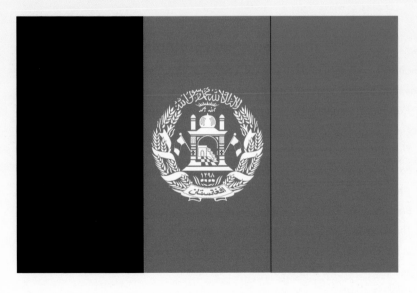

Afghanistan's Flag

Afghanistan's flag consists of vertical stripes of black, red, and green. Black stands for the past, red for bloodshed, and green for hope and prosperity. In the middle of the red stripe is a mosque, a sheaf of wheat, and rays of the sun. The flag also includes an Arabic expression, which in English means, "There is no god but God, and Muhammad is his messenger," and the inscription *Allahu Akbar*, meaning "God is great."

Modern Government

Afghanistan has been ruled by conquerors, emperors, shahs, khans, emirs, princes, kings, prime ministers, and presidents. For centuries, as each new ruler was replaced by another, what remained stable were local and tribal governments. In modern times, the various governments, both community-based and national, have endured political assassinations, an extremist organization that rose and fell from power, war, and a long occupation by a foreign superpower. The national government faces enormous challenges in recovering from all of this.

Although some Afghan governments have ruled by oppressing the people, other leaders have tried to establish more democratic governments. In 1964, Zahir Shah established a constitutional monarchy. He called for the loya jirga to enact a set of laws that became the basis of Afghanistan's

Afghanistan's National Anthem

Afghanistan's national anthem was adopted in 2006. Abdul Bari Jahani wrote the words, and Babrak Wassa wrote the music.

> This land is Afghanistan. It is the pride of every Afghan.
> The land of peace, the land of the sword. Its sons are all brave.
> This is the country of every tribe—land of the Baluch, and the Uzbeks,
> Pashtuns, and Hazaras—Turkman and Tajiks with them,
> Arabs and Gojars, Pamirian, Nuristanis,
> Barahawi, and Qizilbash. Also Aimaq, and Pashaye.
> This land will shine forever, like the sun in the blue sky.
> In the chest of Asia, it will remain as the heart forever.
> We will follow the one God. We all say, Allah is great, we all say,
> Allah is great.

constitution. He gave people more civil rights and reduced the authority that he had as king. In 2004, Afghanistan held its first election by popular vote. The democratically elected government was headed by a president, Hamid Karzai.

Hamid Karzai speaks during his inauguration ceremony in 2009.

Branches of Government

Afghanistan is officially known as the Islamic Republic of Afghanistan. Like the United States and Canada, its national government is divided into three branches—executive, legislative, and judicial. Afghanistan also has the loya jirga, an additional government system that has supreme authority during certain situations. The loya jirga is made up of members of the national legislature, leaders of provincial and district councils, tribal chiefs, and justices of the Supreme Court.

AFGHANISTAN'S NATIONAL GOVERNMENT

Executive Branch
PRESIDENT
VICE PRESIDENTS

Legislative Branch
NATIONAL ASSEMBLY
HOUSE OF ELDERS   HOUSE OF THE PEOPLE

Judicial Branch
SUPREME COURT
APPEALS COURTS
PRIMARY COURTS

Its role is to make decisions on the most vital issues, such as protecting national boundaries, preserving the authority of the government, changing the constitution, and putting the president on trial. In the constitution, the loya jirga is called "the highest manifestation of the will of the people of Afghanistan."

Executive Branch

A president and two vice presidents lead the executive branch. The Afghan people elect the president to a five-year term. The president appoints cabinet ministers, who must be approved by the legislature. The president also appoints one-third of the upper house of the legislature, called the House of Elders. He must make sure to include two representatives who are disabled, and two who represent the impoverished nomadic minority, the Kuchis. Fifty percent of the president's selections must be women. The president also appoints provincial governors for each of the thirty-four provinces in Afghanistan.

Legislative Branch

The legislative branch of the government is called the National Assembly. It is made up of two branches: the House of Elders and the House of the People. The House of the People has

a maximum of 250 members. Sixty-eight of them must be women, generally two from each province. Members of the House of the People are elected directly by Afghan citizens, and each member serves a five-year term. The House of Elders has 102 members. Those not appointed by the president are selected by provincial and district councils. Some members have four-year terms, and some have three-year terms.

The National Assembly is responsible for making laws and approving treaties with other countries. It also confirms declarations of war made by the president and gives permission to send troops abroad.

By law, the Afghan legislature must include women. Two women ran for president in 2009.

Kabul: Afghanistan's Capital City

Kabul has been Afghanistan's capital since 1776. The city was founded more than 3,500 years ago. With about two million residents, it is the nation's largest city. Like Afghanistan as a whole, the city has been invaded frequently over the centuries. Many of the city's finest buildings are in ruin after years of war. But the city is trying to rebuild. The old part of Kabul is filled with lively markets lining narrow streets. The National Museum of Afghanistan holds many treasures, some dating back to the days before Islam came to the country. Much was stolen during the years of chaos in the 1990s, and only some of it has been recovered.

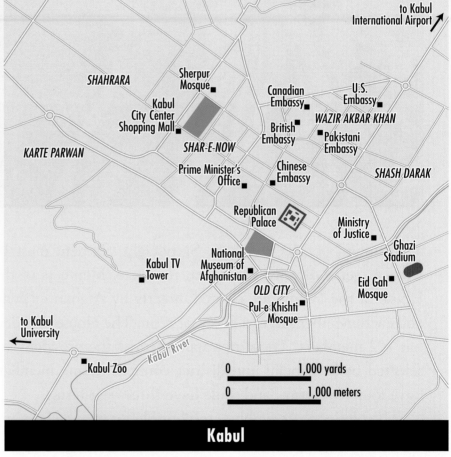

Kabul

Afghanistan has a Supreme Court with nine justices. The president appoints the justices for ten-year terms, although the House of the People has to approve his or her appointments. In the United States, justices serve until they want to retire, but in Afghanistan, a justice cannot serve more than ten years. The Supreme Court has four parts. Each is headed by a justice who has special knowledge in a certain area of law.

Directly below the Supreme Court is the Appeals Court, which hears cases that have already been tried in lower courts. The primary courts, or provincial trial courts, are the largest part of the judicial system. Afghanistan also has local courts, including those at the district, municipal, and village levels, and tribal councils.

Afghanistan is an Islamic state, and shari'a, or Islamic law, is an important part of the judicial system. Shari'a law comes from four main sources: the teachings of the Prophet Muhammad in the Qur'an; the Hadith, which are the recorded sayings and actions of the Prophet; fatwas, which are rulings made by Islamic scholars; and consensus, or *shura* law.

Shura

Shura is one of the four principles of Islamic justice. It means "mutual consultation." In other words, decisions become final only after people have had a chance to share their ideas and opinions. In communities throughout Afghanistan, people attend shura meetings and discuss their common needs and the means to attain them. Everyone's point of view is heard, and once a decision has been reached, all agree to accept the outcome.

A meeting begins with a prayer. People are expected to study the topic beforehand, and at the meeting, people must listen closely and not interrupt or be sarcastic. If others do not like an opinion, the speaker must accept rejection gracefully and obey the final decision.

The Marketplace

A FTER YEARS OF WAR, AFGHANISTAN NEEDS TO rebuild. Progress is happening, but it is slow. The country has exhausted a great deal of its own financial resources, but many nations around the world are donating money, ideas, and people to help Afghanistan move forward.

Opposite: **A young man sells rugs at a market in Afghanistan.**

Agriculture

Agriculture has been one of the fastest-growing areas of improvement in the country. The majority of the population works in agriculture. The money donated by other countries has allowed Afghans to improve the variety and quality of crops they grow. It has also paid for new, more efficient farming technology. Improvements include seeds that produce more food, fertilizers to help plants grow, and updated irrigation systems.

Besides food grown to sell to local markets, Afghan farmers are expanding the crops they grow for export. These include apples, apricots, melons, and grapes. In 2010, Afghanistan exported 170,000 tons (155,000 metric tons) of apples to

In 2010, Afghanistan produced 3.4 million tons of wheat.

India, Pakistan, and the United Arab Emirates. Afghans take special pride in the dozens of varieties of raisins they produce. Exports of fruits are rapidly increasing.

Weights and Measures

Afghanistan uses the metric system. Fruits, meats, and vegetables in the marketplace are sold by the kilogram (2.2 pounds). Items sold by length, such as lumber or cloth, are measured in meters (3.3 feet). Speed is measured by kilometers per hour, which equals 0.6 miles per hour.

What Afghanistan Grows, Makes, and Mines

Agriculture (2008)

Wheat	2,623,000 metric tons
Rice	410,000 metric tons
Grapes	350,000 metric tons

Manufacturing (2006, value added in afghanis)

Food products	48,575,000,000
Chemicals	1,206,000,000
Construction materials	809,000,000

Mining

Natural gas (2006)	20,000,000 cubic meters
Salt (2009)	158,218 metric tons
Chromite (2007)	6,800 metric tons

Opium Production

Farmers throughout Afghanistan must contend with frequent droughts and plant-destroying pests. But even in the worst of conditions, opium poppies—the plant from which the drugs opium and heroin are made—almost always thrive. Growing opium poppies is illegal, but they are easy to plant, grow, harvest, and sell. Villagers who once farmed fields of grain and raised fruit in the orchards now grow poppies instead, and make ten to twenty times more money. Opium poppy fields can be found in nearly every province in Afghanistan.

Workers pick crocus flowers, which produce a spice called saffron.

The national government and international agencies are working to reduce poppy production, but they understand that this crop raises the standard of living in poor villages. Some of their programs have worked, such as improving roads to markets so it is easier for villagers to sell their legal crops. Farmers have also been given money to not grow poppies. But the drug dealers are powerful and put pressure on farmers to supply them with opium. They give the farmers the funds they need to buy fertilizers and farm equipment. Experts believe that Afghanistan produces most of the world's illegal opium and that opium production is the single largest industry in the country.

The second most valuable crop in Afghanistan is saffron, a flower grown for dyes and spices. The Afghan government and international aid groups are encouraging farmers to grow saffron. They are also helping farmers increase food production in general. For example, in Herat, nurseries have been developed to improve the health of trees and to expand the size of orchards that produce pine nuts, almonds, and pistachios. Raising livestock, such as sheep, goats, horses, yaks, and cattle, is another major part of traditional agriculture. Over the

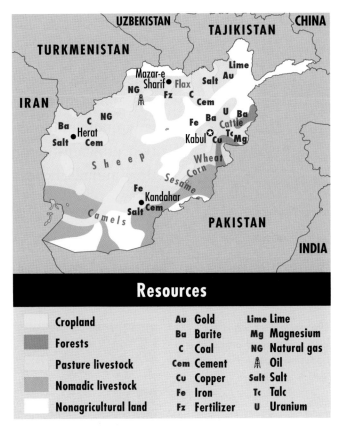

Resources

Cropland		Au	Gold	Lime	Lime
Forests		Ba	Barite	Mg	Magnesium
Pasture livestock		C	Coal	NG	Natural gas
Nomadic livestock		Cem	Cement	Å	Oil
Nonagricultural land		Cu	Copper	Salt	Salt
		Fe	Iron	Tc	Talc
		Fz	Fertilizer	U	Uranium

Money Facts

The Afghan unit of currency is the afghani, which is divided into 100 puls. Coins come in values of 1, 2, and 5 afghanis. Bills come in values of 1, 2, 5, 10, 20, 50, 100, 500, and 1,000. In 2011, 45 afghanis equaled one U.S. dollar.

Afghani bills are quite colorful. The 1,000-Afghani bill, for example, is colored orange and rose. The front shows an image of the Blue Mosque in Mazar-e Sharif. The back shows the tomb of Ahmad Shah Durrani.

past decade, successful programs have helped herders and ranchers to boost feed production, extend rangelands in an environmentally responsible way, and offer veterinary education programs in rural areas that teach people how to keep their animals healthy.

Service Industries

Service industries are a large part of the economy. Although the numbers vary greatly, some people estimate that service workers account for 40 percent of the nation's legal income. Service

The city of Herat has a long tradition of producing beautiful glass.

At one time, Afghanistan was a tourist destination for travelers who wanted to experience a rich culture and dramatic landscape. When Marco Polo journeyed through Afghanistan in the thirteenth century, he found "fine country all the way, thickly peopled and rich in fruit, grain, and vines." In the not-so-distant past, mountaineers came from all over the world to climb the Hindu Kush and Pamir Mountains. Other tourists visited Afghanistan for its ancient architecture, religious shrines, and history, and to explore the Silk Road. But three decades of war have changed that. Many Afghans hope that as the country rebuilds, tourism will once again be a part of the economy.

workers do not manufacture a product. Instead, they provide services such as selling goods in a store, cleaning houses, driving taxis and buses, or doing office work. Higher-paying service workers are employed in banking, insurance, education, health care, social work, technology, and entertainment.

Manufacturing

Afghanistan's first factories were established in the 1920s. They made cotton and woolen cloth, soap, shoes, pottery, and furniture. But Afghanistan did not become an industrial country. Today, Afghanistan manufactures some goods, such as cloth, furniture, and construction materials. For the most part, however, Afghans rely on imports from other countries. But crafts such as leatherwork, pottery, metalwork, and baskets are made by skilled local craftspeople. Most famous of all

The Right Wool

Carpets are one of Afghanistan's most important products. The wool comes from five different types of sheep. The most favored is the Karakul sheep, a hardy breed that can withstand temperatures from 22°F (–5.5°C) to 118°F (48°C). The leading producers of high-quality carpets are the Turkomans, who live in the north. Sheep are sheared in both spring and fall, but the superior wool comes from the spring shearing, as the wool has grown longer and thicker after seven months of winter. Turkoman carpet makers have a custom of putting a match to a piece of the fringe on a finished carpet. They make a wish that the carpet will sell for a good price as quickly as the wool catches fire.

of Afghanistan's artisans are the expert carpet weavers, who create magnificent rugs that are sold around the world.

Mining

Afghanistan has great mineral wealth. Some successful mines produce salt, natural gas, chromite, gemstones, copper, coal, and oil. Like the rest of the economy, war has damaged the mining industry, and in many areas, the ore deposits are difficult to reach. However, mining shows promise for the future. The Afghan Ministry of Mines stated that deposits of chrome, zinc, lead, gold, copper, silver, uranium, and lithium are worth an estimated US$3 trillion. Australia, China, India, and the United States are interested in helping Afghanistan develop its mineral resources by constructing mines and processing plants, and building ways to transport the ore.

Salt is sometimes mined in large pieces. It is then broken up into the tiny crystals commonly used around the world.

Lapis Lazuli

For seven thousand years, a gemstone called lapis lazuli has been mined in Afghanistan's Kokcha River valley. Afghanistan lapis lazuli is known as the world's finest. Kings have coveted it since ancient times. The stone is a deep, rich blue and is used in jewelry, mosaics, and furniture inlays. It has also been ground into powder to be used in medicine and as an ingredient in the natural oil paint called ultramarine. Lapis lazuli from Afghanistan was discovered among the treasures of King Tutankhamen's tomb in ancient Egypt.

A worker keeps an eye on the controls of a hydroelectric plant near Kabul.

Another important project that could add billions of dollars to the Afghan economy is a natural gas pipeline, called the Trans-Afghanistan Pipeline, or TAPI, that would be similar to the oil pipeline that runs from Alaska to the lower forty-eight states in the United States. The pipeline would bring natural gas from Turkmenistan to Pakistan and India, by crossing through Afghanistan.

Energy

Switching on a light or turning on the television is not something people in Afghanistan take for granted. The flow of electricity has been severely disrupted by years of war. Bombs have destroyed many power lines and hydroelectric dams, which are extremely expensive to repair and rebuild. Nearly 90 percent of Afghans in rural areas have little or no electricity. People in cities can lose power for days or weeks at a time.

Electricity in Afghanistan is generated by small coal- and gas-fired power plants in some regions, but most electricity comes from hydroelectric power. There are major dams on the Helmand River, and others near Jalalabad, Kandahar, and Kabul. There are three dams that supply electricity to Kabul, but only one, the Naghlu Dam, has enough water year-round. The cities of Mazar-e Sharif and Herat must buy electricity from Turkmenistan.

With the help of other nations, the Afghan government has been building new and more efficient power plants, and extending and improving power lines. The economic growth of the country depends on gaining access to electric power. It is one of the nation's central goals.

Alternative Energy

Alternative energy such as solar and wind power can help provide electricity to people in remote areas. It does less harm to the environment than using coal, oil, or natural gas. The first wind-powered energy plant in Afghanistan is in the spectacular Panjshir Valley, northeast of Kabul.

A Rich Heritage

Persons per square mile		Persons per square kilometer
more than 518		more than 200
260–518		100–200
65–259		25–99
25–64		10–24
3–24		1–9
fewer than 3		fewer than 1

Like the United States and Canada, Afghanistan is a diverse land. The country is home to more than twenty ethnic groups, and each group is divided into many different tribes, clans, and extended families.

The approximately thirty million Afghans speak more than forty different languages. In 1936, Zahir Shah, in an attempt to unite his country, declared that Pashto would be Afghanistan's official language. However, only about one-third of the people spoke Pashto, so in 1964, Dari became the second official language of Afghanistan. Dari is closely related to the Persian language spoken in Iran. Dari is taught in schools and used in business, and more than half of the population speaks Dari. Many people speak two or more languages, including Uzbek, Turkoman, Nuristani, and Baluchi.

Opposite: **A girl from the Aimaq ethnic group holds a baby. More than 42 percent of Afghans are under age fifteen.**

A Rich Heritage **83**

Nearly all Afghans are Muslim. There are two major sects, or groups, of Islam: Sunni and Shia. Most Afghans are Sunni.

Pashtuns

Forty-two percent of Afghans are Pashtuns, making them the country's largest ethnic group. Their primary language is Pashto, and they are Sunni Muslims. Most Pashtuns live in the south. Their tribal lands cover a sweeping arc from the Pakistan border to just outside of Herat.

There are dozens of tribal divisions among the Pashtuns, and some are enemies of one another. The two largest tribes are the Ghilzai and the Durrani. There is a saying that the Ghilzai have the sword, and the Durrani have the state. The Ghilzai live in the rugged eastern mountains near the Pakistan border and between Kandahar and Kabul. It is a difficult area to farm, and many Ghilzai are poor. They are a tightly knit,

Ethnic Afghanistan	
Pashtun	42%
Tajik	27%
Hazara	9%
Uzbek	9%
Aimaq	4%
Turkoman	3%
Baluchi	2%
Other	4%

sometimes fierce people, who protect their families and villages, and value independence, military skill, and fearless leadership. Many Ghilzai men support the Taliban. Mullah Omar, for instance, is a Ghilzai.

The Durrani live farther west, on the farmland near the Helmand River. For centuries, they have been a part of the ruling elite. The last king of Afghanistan, Zahir Shah, and the nation's first president, Mohammad Daoud, were Durrani Pashtuns, as is the first democratically elected president, Hamid Karzai.

The Pashtuns share a common belief in a code of ethics called Pashtunwali, meaning "the way of the Pashtun." The code outlines how people should act toward each other. For example, it is important to share and be welcoming. When there are conflicts, people should turn to the village loya jirga councils for answers to their problems. The code also describes Pashtun virtues such as courage, protecting one's honor, and respecting the wisdom of the tribe's elders.

Tribal members discuss important issues at the local loya jirga councils.

Many Tajiks are farmers and herders.

Tajiks

The Tajiks first settled along the northern banks of the Amu Darya. They originally came from Iran and are Dari-speaking Sunni Muslims. Near the end of the nineteenth century, the country of Tajikistan was formed, splitting the Tajik tribes. Most chose to live in Tajikistan, but those who remained in Afghanistan became the country's largest minority. In the 1990s, civil war broke out in Tajikistan, and thousands more fled over the border into Afghanistan.

Tajiks have stronger family ties than tribal ones. Most Tajiks live in the north and northeast, where they are farmers and sheepherders. Some make a yearly migration into the mountains to harvest what are often considered the finest nuts and melons in the country. Other Tajiks are urban dwellers. Kabul was once the heart of their community, until 1776 when the son of Ahmad Shah Durrani declared that Kabul was the new Pashtun capital. During the battle against the Taliban, Tajiks joined the Northern Alliance in great numbers. In Kabul today, many Tajiks are well-to-do. They often work in business or government service.

Hazaras

The Hazara people are the third-largest ethnic group in Afghanistan. For centuries, the Hazaras have been treated the worst of all the ethnic groups. Many believe the Hazaras are descendants of the Mongol army of one thousand soldiers who invaded Afghanistan in the thirteenth century. *Hazara* means "one thousand" in Persian. The Hazaras' traditional homeland

Hazaras are likely descended from the Mongols. Most live in central Aghanistan.

is in the central highlands, in an area called Hazarajat, which covers Bamiyan and other provinces. Most Hazaras speak Hazaragi, a Persian language mixed with Turkic and Mongol words. Many also speak Dari, as well as Pashto and Baluchi.

The Hazara people are mostly Shia Muslims. Since the eighteenth century, they have been persecuted by Pashtun rulers, who are passionate Sunni Muslims. Pashtuns have forced the Hazaras out of areas such as the Kandahar, Bamiyan, and Helmand provinces.

Traditionally, Hazaras are poor. The climate of Hazarajat can be harsh, roads are inferior, jobs are few, and the rocky, dry terrain makes it difficult to earn a living growing crops. At times, as many as 40 percent of Hazara men have left Hazarajat to work in low-paying jobs in Kabul.

In 2001, when the Taliban were defeated, the plight of the Hazaras improved. Many moved to Kabul, where they now make up almost 25 percent of the population. Education is important to the Hazaras. Both boys and girls are passing entrance exams to the best universities. Many Hazaras are enlisted in the Afghan army and have high-ranking positions. In the past, Hazaras came to Kabul to work in service jobs, but many are now advancing into better-paying jobs in business and government.

Uzbeks

Uzbeks make up about 6 percent of the population. Their ancestry is a mix of Turkic tribes and Mongols. Their Uzbeki language mixes elements of Turkic and Mongolian languages,

Population of Major Cities (2006 est.)

City	Population
Kabul	1,925,548
Kandahar	468,200
Herat	397,465
Mazar-e Sharif	375,181
Kunduz	347,450

and borrows words from Russian and Arabic. Uzbeks also speak Dari and are Sunni Muslims. In Afghanistan, Uzbeks live mainly in the north, occupying parts of what was once the Bactrian Empire. Traditionally farmers and herders, Uzbeks are also active in the marketplace, where they are successful businesspeople and skilled artisans.

Turkomans

The Turkomans were originally nomads from central Asia who settled in northern Afghanistan between Balkh and Herat. They are Sunni Muslims and speak Turkoman, a Turkic language, which also contains some Russian words. In the nineteenth century, Russians began to overrun Turkistan, and many Turkoman people, resenting Russian attitudes toward Islam, fled to Afghanistan. The Turkomans now represent about 3 percent of the population. Turkomans are the shepherds who introduced the prized Karakul sheep to Afghanistan. They produce fine carpets and jewelry, as well as Karakul pelts, coats, and hats.

Turkoman women sometimes wear elaborate hats.

The Meaning of a Hat

Afghanistan's first democratically elected leader, Hamid Karzai, was born a Durrani Pashtun. When he became president, he wanted to show that he was the president of all the people, so instead of wearing his Pashtun turban, he chose to wear a custom-made Karakul hat in public. A Karakul hat is made from the hide of a newborn Karakul lamb. It is traditionally worn by Afghanistan's northern tribes, the Uzbeks, Tajiks, and Turkomans.

Other Groups

Other ethnic groups are also part of Afghan culture. Many of them are nomadic or seminomadic. These include the Aimaq, Baluchi, Kuchi, Kyrgyz, and Wakhi.

The Dari-speaking Aimaq are Sunni Muslims who live in the area around Herat. Aimaq women are given stronger roles in society than are women in many other tribes. The Baluchi are Sunni Muslims living in southern Afghanistan who speak Baluchi, a language that blends Persian, Arabic, and Sindhi, which is spoken by many people in Pakistan.

The approximately three million Kuchis belong to the Ghilzai Pashtun tribal group. As nomads, they travel over vast distances. One of their historical roles was to deliver messages and spread news around the country. Recently, they have been supporters of the Taliban and have carried on many territorial battles with the Hazaras.

The Kyrgyz and Wakhi nomads live mostly in the Pamir Mountains and the Wakhan Corridor. They are herders who raise cattle, horses, sheep, and goats. They live in yurts, which are round tents made of felt and animal hides. They carry the yurts with them when they move from valley to valley.

The Kyrgyz are isolated from the rest of Afghanistan, so their language and customs are more distinct. They are Sunni Muslim, but follow fewer Islamic customs than other Afghan Sunnis. They speak Kyrgyz, a Turkic language.

Wooden poles serve as the framework for the yurts used by the Kyrgyz people.

The Wakhi tribe is equally isolated. Wakhis speak an ancient Persian language and follow a small Islamic sect called Shia Ismaili Islam. The sect's spiritual head is the Aga Khan, a wealthy leader who contributes millions of dollars in aid to Afghanistan each year.

Two other unique groups in Afghanistan are the Qizilbash and the Nuristani. The Qizilbash speak Dari and practice a form of Islam called Imami Shia. Although they are of the minority Shia Muslim population, the nature of their belief allows them to follow the religious practices of those around them to avoid persecution. In Afghanistan, the Qizilbash people are usually city dwellers with professional careers.

The Nuristani people are also distinct. Some claim their ancestry is tied to Alexander the Great, because many Nuristanis have more European-looking features and coloring than other Afghans. Some have blond or red hair, and blue or green eyes. The people speak Nuristani, a language spoken nowhere else. It is related to an ancient Persian language and Sanskrit, an ancient Indian language. Nuristanis live isolated from each other in rugged narrow valleys, and each valley has its own version of the language. A Nuristani is often unable to understand the speech of another Nuristani from a different valley.

Language in Afghanistan

Nearly all languages in Afghanistan are written using the Arabic alphabet. Arabic is written from right to left on the page. Arabic has been translated into the Roman alphabet, in which English is written, in different ways through the years. For example, the word *Qur'an* has been spelled "Quran" and "Koran."

Here are some useful words and phrases in Pashto, Dari, and Uzbeki:

Sign advertising fish for sale

Pashto

As-salaamu' alaykum	Hello
Tsenga yee?	How are you?
Sheh yem	I am well
Luftan	Please
Tashakor	Thank you
Ta da kom zaee ye?	Where are you from?
Za da _____ yem	I am from _____

Dari

Salaam aalaikum	Hello
Lutfan	Please
Tashakur	Thank you
Havayakh zadeh	It's freezing (weather)
Hava garm ast	It's hot (weather)

Uzbeki

Assalomu alaykum!	Hello!
Vaalajkum assalom!	Hello to you, too!
Siz qay yerdansiz?	Where are you from?
Men _____	I'm from _____
Bir til bilish kamlik qiladi	One language is never enough
Yahshi ishlang!	Have a nice day!

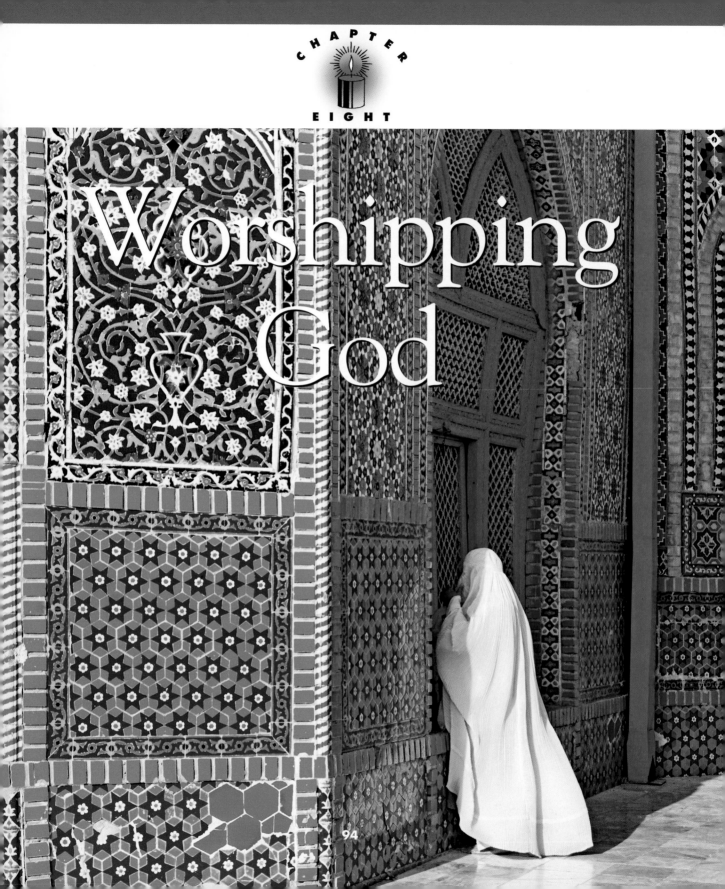

Worshipping God

W HEN CONQUERORS AND INVADERS BROUGHT ISLAM to Afghanistan, the people gave up the traditions of their ancient civilization and adopted the new religious faith. Since its introduction, Afghans have relied on Islam to comfort and guide them through their lives.

The Prophet

Around the year 570 CE, the Prophet Muhammad was born in the small village of Mecca in what is now Saudi Arabia. Muhammad was orphaned at a young age, and he was raised by his grandfather and uncle in Mecca. As was the custom for well-to-do families, the boy was sent to live with a poor Bedouin family. The Bedouin were nomads who moved their herds and belongings from place to place through the harsh deserts. Muhammad developed respect for the poor and learned to admire the Bedouins' patience and hard work. When he returned to his family, Muhammad grew very thoughtful. He often left the village and ventured into the mountains, resting in hidden caves to meditate.

Religions in Afghanistan	
Sunni Muslim	80%
Shia Muslim	19%
Other (Jewish, Hindu, Sikh, Christian, etc.)	1%

Muslims believe that the Qur'an includes all the messages that God gave to Muhammad.

After a time, he began to have religious experiences. He believed God—"Allah" in Arabic—was speaking to him. Many people responded to his words and ideas, and soon Muhammad became known as Allah's messenger. The new religion was called Islam, and its followers were called Muslims, meaning "ones who submit to God."

Muhammad's revelations were recorded in the Muslim holy book, the Qur'an. The teachings of the Prophet spread quickly across Arabia, gathering passionate believers. But after Muhammad's death in 632, a split occurred among his followers, which created the two main sects of Islam, Shia and Sunni. Shia Muslims believe that only a descendant of Muhammad's cousin, Hazrat Ali, can be the rightful spiritual leader of Islam. Sunni Muslims accept the authority of Islam's other spiritual leaders as well. Over time, the two sects developed their own traditions and rules. Throughout the Muslim world, a rift remains.

Islam first came to Afghanistan with Sunni Muslim Arab conquerors in the seventh century. The Muslim conquerors converted the Afghans to Islam. They translated the Qur'an from Arabic into Persian. After the Arab empire fell to an Iranian conqueror, the Iranians introduced Shia Muslim teachings into parts of Afghanistan. Later in the eighth and ninth centuries, Turkic people migrated into Afghanistan, and they adopted many of the local customs, including the belief in Islam.

Today, about 80 percent of all Afghans are Sunni Muslim and 19 percent are Shia Muslim. The Shias belong to three main ethnic groups: the Hazaras, the Qizilbash, and the Ismailis. Only 1 percent of Afghans are not Muslim. This tiny minority includes Jews, Hindus, Sikhs, and Christians.

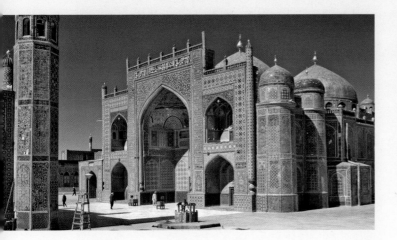

The Blue Mosque

One of the most sacred mosques in all the Muslim world is the Blue Mosque, or the Tomb of the Chosen One, in Mazar-e Sharif. The Chosen One is Hazrat Ali, a cousin of Muhammad, who is supposedly buried there. Although there is serious ethnic and religious discord between Shias and Sunnis in Afghanistan, all ignore their differences to pray together at the Blue Mosque.

Both Sunnis and Shias pray in houses of worship called mosques. The term *mosque* comes from an Arabic word that means "a place of kneeling." There are no seats in a mosque, just open space, with a single podium at the head for the spiritual leader, the mullah. Mats and small prayer rugs cover the floor. It is not permitted to pray to God on an uncovered floor. Muslims pray while kneeling and bowing their heads to the floor.

Friday is the holy day in Islam. Five times a day, a crier called a muezzin climbs a tower called a minaret and calls worshippers to prayer. In communities with large mosques, the muezzin uses a bullhorn to reach out to the faithful.

Minaret of Jam

In a remote location in the Ghur Province, the Minaret of Jam towers 213 feet (65 m) above the Hari River valley. Its true history is unknown, but many scholars think it was built by a Ghurid emperor in the twelfth century. It was so isolated that it was forgotten for many years, until it was rediscovered in 1943 by an airline pilot. The Minaret of Jam, though slightly tilted, is the second-tallest minaret in the world. A striking example of Islamic architecture, it is made of fired clay bricks ornately decorated with blue tiles and inscriptions.

A muezzin calls worshippers to prayer. In some cities, muezzins use loudspeakers.

When the worshippers enter the mosque, they wash their face, hands, and feet, and remove their shoes. The men form rows, shoulder to shoulder, and the women stand behind them. The mullah then gives a sermon. After the sermon, the person in charge of the mosque, called an imam, leads the people in prayer. Together they recite passages from the Qur'an. During prayer, everyone turns in the direction of Mecca, the birthplace of Muhammad. In larger communities and cities, the government usually appoints mullahs. In smaller villages, mullahs have fewer duties and are usually farmers or craftspeople.

The Five Pillars of Islam

Muslims live according to five essential duties, often called the Five Pillars of Islam. The first pillar is *shahada*. This is the center of a Muslim's faith, which is the belief that there is no god but God, and Muhammad is his messenger.

No matter where they are in the world, Muslims always face Mecca when they pray.

The second pillar is *salah*, which says that Muslims should pray five times a day: in the early morning, at noon, in the late afternoon, around sunset, and before going to bed. Before each prayer, Muslims perform a ritual washing, called *wadu*. They wash hands, arms, face, nose, feet, and ankles three times. They rub their heads with water and clean around their ears. Finally, they show that they are ready to pray by lifting their heads and raising a forefinger to the sky. When no pure water is available to cleanse themselves before praying, Muslims can just make the motions of cleaning.

The third pillar is *zakat*, meaning "to purify." This is the belief that Muslims should care for other people and share their wealth. Muslims who give to charity are purifying themselves from greed. Muslims give money to their mosques or their communities to provide food, clothing, or schooling for those in need.

The fourth pillar is *hajj*. All Muslims are supposed to make a pilgrimage to Mecca, the birthplace of Muhammad, once in their lives if they are physically and financially able. A hajj journey has many rituals. Pilgrims wear simple white garments, symbolizing that all people are equals. At historic sites, pilgrims do ceremonial bathing and special praying. Each year, millions of Muslims make their way to Mecca. For a Muslim, performing the hajj is the most honorable act.

The fifth pillar is *saum*. Saum is the celebration of Ramadan, the ninth and holiest month of the year in the Islamic calendar. It was in the ninth month that Muhammad began receiving his messages from God. During Ramadan, Muslims do not eat or drink between sunrise and sunset. This helps remind Muslims how difficult it is to be poor, hungry, and thirsty.

About three million people take part in the hajj pilgrimage to Mecca each year.

A boy dressed in new clothes watches worshippers celebrate 'Id al-Fitr. Many Muslims get new clothes for this celebration.

Holidays

Most holidays in Afghanistan are religious holidays. 'Id al-Fitr is celebrated for three days at the end of Ramadan. Afghans have a unique way of celebrating 'Id al-Fitr. At sunset, men gather in public squares to play cards and games. They dress in their finest clothes and outline their eyes with kohl (a charcoal-like substance). All the men bring hard-boiled eggs and throw them, trying to break each others' eggs.

Another important holiday is 'Id al-Adha, which means the "feast of sacrifice." It commemorates the sacrifice that

Abraham was willing to make to show his love for God. As the story goes, God asked Abraham to kill his only son to prove his faith. With a heavy heart, Abraham climbed a mountain with his son and placed him on an altar. God saw that Abraham was willing to make the ultimate sacrifice, so he replaced Abraham's son with a sacrificial goat.

To celebrate their faith in God, Muslims rise early on the morning of 'Id al-Adha. They dress in their best clothes and have a community prayer. Then people sacrifice a goat, which must be young and healthy. Poor families share the cost of a goat. While the goat is being sacrificed, people recite a special prayer. Afterward, family and friends come together to share a meal and greet each other by saying, "May Allah accept good deeds from us and from you."

Other Faiths

Nearly all Hindus, Sikhs, Jews, and Christians in Afghanistan live in Kabul or other major cities. They are not publicly active in their religious practices. Hinduism is an ancient religion founded in India. Hindus worship many gods, such as Shiva or Krishna. This is in contrast to Muslims, Jews, Sikhs, and Christians, who believe in only one god. The Sikh religion is a blend of Hinduism and Islam. When the Taliban came to power, they persecuted Hindus and Sikhs, making them hang yellow cloth outside of their homes to mark them as non-Muslims. Once the Taliban lost power, Sikhs and Hindus were allowed to leave the country and settle elsewhere. Many did, leaving even fewer religious minorities in Afghanistan.

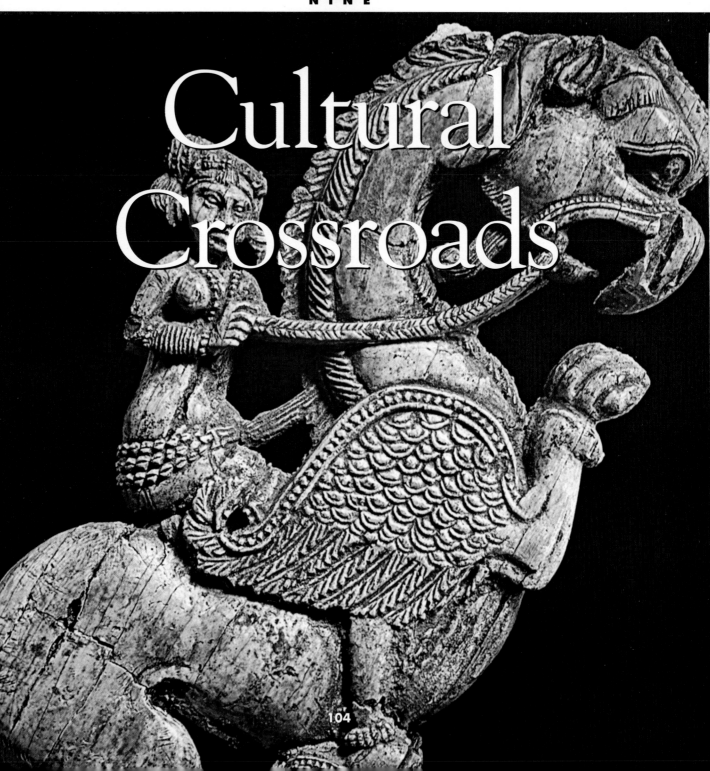

Cultural Crossroads

F AR TOO OFTEN, STORIES ABOUT AFGHANISTAN AND its people involve never-ending struggle. But in spite of poverty and hardship, oppression and war, Afghans have created, and fiercely protect, a rich and unique culture.

Painting and Sculpture

Oil painting was thought to have been invented in Europe in the fifteenth century, but the first oil paintings were actually made in Afghanistan eight hundred years earlier. After the Taliban blew up the large Buddha statues in Bamiyan, archaeologists explored inside the caves where the Buddhas had stood. In 2008, they discovered what had been hidden from view for fourteen centuries—the world's first oil paintings. The paintings are murals showing images of Buddha dressed in flowing red robes sitting with mythical creatures under palm leaves and lush flowers. The oil paints themselves were likely made from oils extracted from wild walnuts and poppy seeds.

The earliest known Afghan sculptures were statues created in Kandahar in the first century CE. At the time, Kandahar was

The caves that held the Bamiyan Buddhas contained ancient oil paintings.

a major crossroads for trade and culture. Art and sculpture from the area blended styles of Roman, Greek, and Indian art. The Kandahar statues were fashioned of painted clay. Sculptors created images of the Indian Buddha with a Roman or Greek face surrounded by classic Roman designs, such as swirling vines, cherubs wearing flowers, and centaurs—the mythical creatures with the head of a man and the body of a horse.

During the twelfth and thirteenth centuries, metalwork flourished in Herat. Artists made practical items such as water jugs, candlesticks, bowls, and inkwells that were beautifully decorated with images of humans and animals. They inlaid the designs onto bands of silver, copper, gems, and gold.

Painting in miniature is another style of Afghan art that came from Herat. The greatest miniaturist, Kamal ad-Din

Bihzad, lived in the fifteenth century. He painted hunting scenes, elegant princes, and sleeping maidens. He used rich colors, especially a deep blue made from crushed lapis lazuli. Bihzad became the director of the Herat Academy and was the first Afghan painter to sign his name to his work. He was such a master that later miniaturists out of respect would only sign their best paintings "Worthy of Bihzad," instead of with their own names.

As Islam became more rooted in Afghan society, the style of art changed. Muslim artists typically do not depict humans or animals because Allah is considered the sole creator. Instead, they draw and paint abstract patterns and shapes. They also do calligraphy—fancy, decorative lettering—using passages from the Qur'an.

Calligraphy, the art of beautiful lettering, is highly valued in Afghanistan.

Saving Art

With its long history of invasions, Afghans have needed to protect their art from raiders and destroyers. People hid ancient treasures in caves or buried them underground. During the Soviet invasion, rockets that were fired into the National Museum of Afghanistan (below) in Kabul destroyed countless objects. Concerned government workers took what objects they could and hid them. Recently, a wealthy art collector tracked down the hidden objects, mostly ancient ivory carvings. He purchased them and donated them back to the National Museum.

During Taliban rule, more than two thousand pieces of valuable Afghan art were damaged or destroyed. The Taliban especially condemned paintings of human figures and animals. An Afghan doctor named Yousef Asefi rescued many paintings. He hid them by painting his own watercolor paintings on top of the originals. When the Taliban fell, Asefi washed his paints away and restored the paintings to their rightful places in galleries and museums.

In 1978, archaeologists stumbled upon a hidden treasure of gold jewelry and other artifacts in an ancient nomad cemetery. The nomads had been royalty, so their possessions were particularly valuable. The most spectacular piece was an elaborate gold crown that could be folded so the nomads could easily transport it. Art experts say it is one of the world's most valuable pieces of art. After the nomad treasures were unearthed, some Afghan officials knew the artifacts would be at risk under Soviet and, later, Taliban rule. They hid the art in locked boxes under the Presidential Palace. The artifacts were not unsealed until 2004, when they were included in an international traveling exhibit of Afghan art.

Today, some Afghan artists are again depicting people. A rising art form in Kabul is called *roshd*, meaning "growth." Roshd is mural or graffiti art that has social themes. Artists use spray paints to depict scenes of everyday life and to criticize modern society in ways they hope will cause a stir and stimulate change. One image on the wall of an old factory shows a broken-down public bus, its wheels missing, full of people stuck on the road. The artist was making a point about the need for better government services. Another painting shows women in burqas coming up from the sea. The artist explained that he wanted strict Muslims to consider the idea that women are as clean and pure as water.

The variety of art in Afghanistan has grown since the end of Taliban rule. The country's first exhibit by female artists was held in 2008.

Much of the music and dance in Afghanistan is based on traditional folk songs, ballads, and dances. Traditional musical instruments include the *rohab*, a stringed instrument similar to a violin or cello; the *santur*, which is like a zither; the *chang*, which is a mouth harp; and drums that are played with the palms and fingers. Recently, Afghan musicians have begun to tour internationally.

The attan is a Pashtun dance. Men often perform it at weddings and other celebrations.

A Man of Many Talents

In 1955, an Afghan musician, painter, and playwright named Abdul Ghafur Breshna founded the Afghan Fine Arts College, which has since become a school that teaches young artists painting, sculpture, drawing, needlework, and jewelry making. He is remembered for his paintings that captured the best of Afghanistan and showed his great love for his country. He painted landscapes and scenic roadways as well as portraits of poets, philosophers, and rulers. Breshna was also a newspaper publisher who introduced color printing technology to the national newspaper.

In addition, Breshna was noted for his music composition and earned the title *Ustad*, meaning "music master." Breshna was once the president of Radio Afghanistan. He was the first person to broadcast a female singer, Mermon Parwin, on the radio. Because of his support, her fame spread, and she was one of the first women to be given the title of Ustad.

The national dance, the *attan*, is of Pashtun origin. It is performed only by men. Dancers stand in a circle around a stake or fire. They clap their hands to the beat of the music, while dancing faster and faster as the music speeds up.

Theater and film are not traditional art forms in Afghanistan, but they were beginning to blossom before the Soviet invasion. Since the fall of the Taliban, small theater companies have been growing in cities such as Herat, Kabul, and Mazar-e Sharif. Some movie houses that were shut down by the Taliban have also been revived.

Architecture

Afghan architecture includes religious monuments, shrines, towers, monasteries, tombs, mosques, and temples. The country's greatest structures include the Friday Mosque in Herat, the Blue Mosque in Mazar-e Sharif, and the Mosque of the Sacred Cloak in Kandahar.

Herat is known for its splendid buildings. Notable buildings besides the Friday Mosque include the Musallah Complex built by Queen Gawhar Shad, her domed tomb, and several towering minarets. Architects in the twelfth through the fifteenth centuries wanted their buildings to be set apart from their surroundings. They began decorating their buildings by cutting up colored tiles and making bright mosaic designs. As a result, the buildings in Herat seemed to glitter as they rose up from the colorless, dreary steppe.

Construction began on the Friday Mosque in Herat in the year 1200.

Sacred Site

The Shrine of Hazrat Ali in Mazar-e Sharif is the most sacred and visited site in Afghanistan. The mosque is magnificently decorated in blue tiles, inside and out. Afghans, both Sunni and Shia, put away their differences to pray together and join in the annual Nawruz festivities celebrating the new year. White doves surround the plaza and fill the skies above the blue tiled dome. Afghans believe the doves are good luck. They say that when the birds fly near, they change color from gray to white because of the holiness of the place. Visitors believe that if a bird lands on their shoulder, they will become lucky, too.

Nearly all of Afghanistan's historic structures have been attacked or looted. Decay and warfare remain causes for concern. The nation's biggest architectural projects, such as the reconstruction of the Friday Mosque, help preserve and rebuild Afghanistan's great architectural heritage.

The Shia Ismaili spiritual leader Aga Khan has established the Aga Khan Trust for Culture in Afghanistan. The trust pays for Afghan architects and craftspeople to renovate homes and historic buildings that have been bombed, abandoned, or neglected.

Literature

The primary form of literature in Afghanistan is poetry. Traditionally, few Afghans have been able to read and write, so stories, epics, and poems were memorized and shared orally. Especially in Herat, leading patrons of the arts encouraged

This illustration in *Book of Kings* depicts paradise on earth. People and animals get along, and there is plenty of fruit, flowers, and water.

poets. In the fifteenth century, a poetry patron joked, "Here in Herat one cannot stretch out a leg without poking a poet in his backside!"

Queen Gawhar Shad also celebrated poetry. One of the poets she supported was Nur ad-Din Abd ar-Rahman Jami, considered Afghanistan's greatest poet. He is known for his thousands of poems and *ghazals*. A ghazal is an ancient form of poetry that contains rhymes, couplets, and refrains set to music. The form is still used today.

One of the world's best-known epic poems is *Book of Kings*, by Ferdausi of Ghazni. It contains sixty thousand rhyming couplets. Another Afghan poet, Rabia Balkhi, was a princess from Balkh. Her life was cut short when she fell in love with her brother's slave. Her brother slashed her with his sword and built a prison around her. She stood up to him by writing her last poem with her own blood on the walls of her cell. Today, many hospitals and schools are named in her honor.

Pashtun women compose a traditional form of poetry. Their poems are two to four lines that describe their daily lives and are often about their husbands. The poems reveal their private sarcasm and humor.

Today, poetry continues to be a part of everyday life in Afghanistan. It is a means for parents and teachers to educate children and share Afghan culture. Books of poetry are found in almost every home, and poetry contests are a popular pastime.

Many writers left Afghanistan in recent decades, seeking literary freedom away from the Soviets and the Taliban. They include Homira Qaderi, who writes about her native Herat, and Khaled Hosseini, who writes about Kabul. Hosseini's book *The Kite Runner* was made into a successful movie in the United States. Because it showed violence and ethnic tensions, however, it was banned in Afghanistan. Writers who live and work in Afghanistan continue to write poetry and short stories in keeping with their ancient traditions; but many now write about social conditions and the need for peace and reconstruction.

Family and Community

116

Most Afghans live in villages. Fewer than 25 percent live in cities, and a small minority are nomads. Regardless of lifestyle, family and home life are the basis for any Afghan community. No matter the differences, the people in each community follow the word of God, practice *halal*, which means the right way to live, and avoid *haram*, which is the wrong way to live.

Life in the Village

More than thirty thousand villages are sprinkled across the country. Many villages are near cities and towns, so that farmers, craftspeople, and merchants can easily get to market to sell their crops, livestock, crafts, and other goods. Other villages are so remote that people have only each other to rely on for food and supplies. Nomads, too, are dependent on each other.

All village life revolves around the family. Typical families have a man as the head of the household, his wife, children, parents, brothers, and unmarried or widowed sisters, aunts, or cousins. Marriage unites families even further, as many men marry their cousins. With such intimate relationships,

Houses in Afghan villages are small and simple.

anything good or bad that happens to one family member is shared by all. A successful sales day at the market for one family member is reason for everyone to celebrate; an insult received by a family member is cause for revenge. Big extended families, or clans, can carry longstanding grudges against other clans, based on actual or imagined slights. Within their clans, family members are intensely loyal.

Village houses are simple. They are small, with walls made of mud and straw, and roofs made of brick. The houses have just a few rooms and humble furnishings, mostly mats, pillows, rugs, and mattresses. Most rooms do double duty as day rooms and sleeping rooms. During the day, sleeping rugs, blankets, and mattresses are piled in a corner. Each house has a *hujra*, or guest room, at the front of the house. Afghans, no matter how poor, always welcome friends, travelers, and even strangers to their home. Families also use the hujra to chat and play games. Houses are heated by fires stoked with wood or dried animal dung. To warm the whole house, tunnels under the floor connect to the fireplace and circulate heat. Electricity and indoor plumbing are rare.

Being so closely knit, people in villages rely on family and local government leaders for guidance and justice. The father is head of the house and holds the ultimate authority over family matters. After his death, the oldest son takes over the role. Women are generally respected for their contributions to the family but do not participate in public life. Each village has three men who oversee the community: the *malik*, who is the local chief; the *mirab*, who manages the water supply; and the mullah, who is the religious leader. Some villagers have a khan, a landowner who acts as both malik and mirab.

City Life

People who live in cities are slightly more independent. They have friends outside of their clans and are less likely to marry a cousin or other relative. Their houses and apartments tend to be more modern. The fortunate even have electricity and plumbing. Kabul, Mazar-e Sharif, and Herat have more modern conveniences and more diversity in their communities; Jalalabad, Kandahar, and Ghazni are more traditional communities.

Yurts typically have a circular wooden frame and a felt covering.

Nomadic Life

Nomads share some, but not all, of the same relationships with family and local government as villagers do. Many nomads work as herders and farmworkers. Women help tend livestock and harvest fruit and nuts side by side with the men. Their labor gives most female nomads a greater role in the community.

Nomads do not have mosques or visit mosques to pray. Most nomads live in yurts. The front door opening of a yurt is covered by a thick woven carpet. Furnishings include pillows, rugs, and blankets. Household goods and utensils are stored in handwoven wool bags and hung on the walls. As nomads travel, they visit established villages and barter for food and other goods. They also bring news from other villages.

Marriage

One of the most critical decisions Afghans make is whom to marry. The groom must choose someone who will maintain or lift his social and economic status. But the bride cannot be too sought after because a groom must pay a bride price—and the more desirable the bride, the higher the price. The bride price is a combination of money, land, and goods that a groom provides to the bride's family. In turn, the bride's family donates useful household items such as rugs, cookware, and clothing to the young couple.

The Wedding

A village wedding is a grand affair, full of joy and ritual. The bride and her female relatives have a henna party on the day before the wedding. Henna is a red-brown vegetable dye used to decorate the skin. Children from the groom's family deliver the henna to the bride. She is dressed in jewels and fine clothing.

On the day of the wedding, the bride and her family wait at home, while the groom and his family and friends have a big luncheon, with musicians playing outside. After the lunch, the groom and his party form a procession to the bride's house. Sometimes he rides a horse. Once he arrives, a mullah gives a short sermon about marriage and its responsibilities.

At the ceremony, the groom's family provides all the guests with tea and food. Two decorated chairs, or a sofa surrounded by candles and flowers, wait for the wedding couple. When they arrive, the guests stand while the two enter together with the Qur'an held over their heads. Once seated, a shawl is draped over the bride and groom, and a mirror is placed between them. They recite passages from the Qur'an. Then everyone celebrates with food, music, dancing, and a wedding cake.

After the wedding, a procession forms to take the bride to her husband's home. The groom's family sacrifices a sheep or goat in her honor. The bride is given a hammer and nail, and as she walks into her husband's home for the first time, she hammers the nail into the doorway, signifying that she has committed herself to her husband.

Years of war and strife have made it difficult for young men to put together an adequate bride price. Men usually marry in their early twenties, and young women in their teens. But because it takes longer today for men to save money, they sometimes fail to earn enough to marry, and young women end up marrying older and richer men.

Clothing

In cities, many people wear Western clothing, or a combination of Western and traditional clothing. But in villages, traditional clothing is typical. Men wear a loose-fitting shirt and vest over loose drawstring pants called *shalwar kameez*. Pashtuns and members of other ethnic groups also wear a skullcap and a turban. Men wind long strips of cloth around their head, leaving their forehead exposed so they can touch it to the ground when praying. Turbans often show what tribe the wearer is from. The Taliban decreed that men wear beards, though many men today are clean-shaven.

Women wear long dresses and a scarf over their head. Some also wear a shawl to cover their face when around strangers. Some women wear a burqa, which covers their entire body and face. During the time of the Taliban, women were required by law to wear a burqa.

Some tribes have distinct styles of dress. Hazara men wear heavier fabrics against the cold, such as wool or thickly woven cotton. Hazara women wear lighter garments because they are usually indoors. Men's clothing is plain colored, but women dress in bright colors and bold designs. Tajik men often wear

Western clothing. Tajik traditional clothing, which is most often worn by older men, includes a long coat and a turban. Because they are farmers and herders, Tajiks wear heavy work boots over their shoes. Uzbek and Turkoman men wear a Karakul hat. This type of hat is made from the pelt of a newborn lamb, and has a silky sheen. Karakul hats can be very expensive and are usually only worn by the well-to-do. Kyrgyz nomad men wear a hat called a *kalpak*, made of four panels of white felt, fur, or wool stitched together. Women wear long skirts and kerchiefs. Traditional clothing for Wakhi men is a coat made from untanned goatskin. Women knit colorful sweaters, hats, and gloves.

A man sells naan at a market in Kunduz, in northern Afghanistan.

Food and Drink

Afghan food is a simple blending of the many cultures of the land. A typical Afghan kitchen is basic. Few people have ovens, even those who live in the city. Instead, they cook over wood or charcoal fires. The staple foods are rice, noodles, and naan, a flat bread baked in clay pots buried underground. Most meals are composed of *pilau*, which is mildly spiced rice mixed with meat and vegetables. Naan is generally used as an eating utensil. If a person has no bread, the food is scooped up with the right hand. Dessert is often fruit or a puddinglike dish made from bread or rice. Tea is the universal drink. Even small villages have at least one teahouse, where men gather to sit and talk. In cities, teahouses abound.

Having Fun

Afghans do not have a lot of money, so pastimes are simple. In spring, families especially enjoy picnics. *Gudiparan bazi*, or kite flying, is the national pastime, and is often the focus of a picnic. Kite flying is also a serious competitive sport among boys. Great honor is bestowed on the winners. Competitive kite flying requires a team of two, one to fly the kite and the other to hold a spool of wire. Kites can be any size, and they are made painstakingly. The word for *kite* means "flying doll." The kite is attached to a wire coated with ground glass mixed with paste. Once two kites are aloft and their wires touch, the fighting begins. The winner is the person who cuts the wire of the other kite, causing it to fly off in the wind. Boys race to the fallen kite to claim it as their own.

Sports played by men are fiercely competitive. One is a type of wrestling called *pehlwani*. Men confront each other, and the rules allow them to attack by grabbing clothing, as well as arms and legs. The clothes of both wrestlers are typically hanging in shreds at the end of a match. Another popular sport is called *buzkashi*, which means "get the goat." In this sport, teams of men on horseback circle around the body of a dead goat. At a signal, they rush in and try to drag the goat onto their horses. Once a player has gotten the goat, he

races toward the goal, while the opposing players try to snatch the goat away.

Buzkashi is an intense and dangerous game.

Health and Education

Health care in Afghanistan has been in crisis for many years. Under Soviet and Taliban rule, many educated Afghans left the country, leaving few trained medical workers. Under the Taliban, women were not allowed to work. This harmed health care for women, because in Afghanistan, women can only be treated by a female doctor or nurse. The nation has one of the lowest life expectancies in the world, averaging less than forty-five years. One in five children dies before the age of five. Clinics and hospitals lack many basics, such as access to a clean water supply, reliable electricity, and modern medical equipment. Medicines are rarely available in

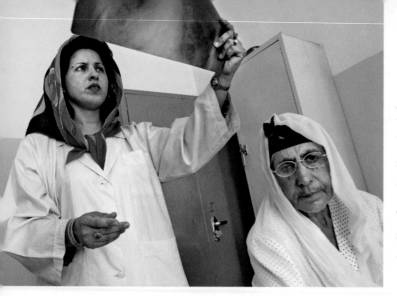

A doctor studies an X-ray at a hospital in Kabul. Under the Taliban, women were not allowed to be doctors.

hospitals. Instead, family members must purchase medicine elsewhere and bring it back to the hospital for the patient. Especially in villages, curable diseases go untreated. In addition, roads are bad, so transportation to medical centers is difficult.

Improvements are being made. The Afghan Ministry of Health has established a public health care system and is supporting more education and training for doctors and other health care workers, especially women doctors. International aid organizations are donating money and providing trained workers to help expand and improve medical care for all Afghans.

Education is another area that is only slowly improving. Afghans have a low literacy rate—only about 25 percent of women and 55 percent of men can read and write. Many children do not attend school. Those who do go to school attend from March to November, six days a week. Education used to be provided by village mullahs who taught the Qur'an to students. During Taliban rule, girls were not allowed to go to school, although some women risked their lives to hold

Happy New Year

The Persian New Year festival is the most beloved holiday in Afghanistan. Called Nawruz, meaning "new day," the festival takes place on March 21, at the beginning of spring. During Nawruz, people enjoy holiday foods, dancing, and music. An unusual Nawruz activity in Afghanistan is the custom of dyeing farm animals. Nawruz carnivals feature blue chickens, purple goats, and green sheep.

secret classes for girls. Today, the Afghan government, with the help of international aid money and workers, is building more elementary schools throughout the country. In 2000, Afghanistan had 800,000 schoolchildren, most of them boys. Today, there are more than 8.5 million children in school, including 2.5 million girls.

Toward the Future

Afghanistan is a complex place. In some areas, life goes on as it has for centuries. In other areas, there is warfare. In cities, there is a growing modern Afghan style. Democracy and peace are important goals for many people. Afghanistan has experienced chaos for much of its long history. Afghans are striving for stability and a better standard of living for people across the nation.

In Afghanistan, girls and boys attend separate schools.

Timeline

Afghanistan History		World History	
Aryans establish the kingdom of Ariana.	ca. 1500 BCE	ca. 2500 BCE Egyptians build the pyramids and the Sphinx in Giza.	
Cyrus the Great conquers Ariana.	540 BCE	ca. 563 BCE The Buddha is born in India.	
Alexander the Great captures Kandahar and Herat.	328 BCE	313 CE The Roman emperor Constantine legalizes Christianity.	
The Kushans conquer Bactria.	ca. 150 BCE		
The Sassanids take over Afghanistan.	241 CE		
Islam is introduced into Afghanistan.	642	610 The Prophet Muhammad begins preaching a new religion called Islam.	
Mahmud of Ghazni creates the first Afghan Empire.	998		
		1054 The Eastern (Orthodox) and Western (Roman Catholic) Churches break apart.	
		1095 The Crusades begin.	
Genghis Khan and the Mongols conquer Afghanistan.	1219	1215 King John seals the Magna Carta.	
		1300s The Renaissance begins in Italy.	
		1347 The plague sweeps through Europe.	
Timur establishes his empire.	1370		
		1453 Ottoman Turks capture Constantinople, conquering the Byzantine Empire.	
		1492 Columbus arrives in North America.	
Babur, the founder of the Moghul Empire, conquers Kabul.	1504	1500s Reformers break away from the Catholic Church, and Protestantism is born.	
Ahmad Shah Durrani establishes the Durrani dynasty.	1747	1776 The U.S. Declaration of Independence is signed.	
		1789 The French Revolution begins.	
Dost Mohammad Khan becomes ruler of Afghanistan.	1826		
The First Anglo-Afghan War begins.	1839		

Afghanistan History

The Second Anglo-Afghan War begins.	1878
The Third Anglo-Afghan War is fought; Afghanistan declares independence from Britain.	1919
Afghanistan's first constitution is drafted.	1923
Muhammad Zahir Shah takes power.	1933
Zahir Shah draws up a new constitution.	1964
Soviet troops invade Afghanistan.	1979
The Soviets withdraw from Afghanistan.	1989
Ahmad Shah Massoud and the mujahidin take over Kabul.	1992
The Taliban gain control of Afghanistan.	1996
Al-Qaeda terrorists, supported by the Taliban, attack New York City and Washington, D.C. In retaliation, U.S. forces and the Northern Alliance topple the Taliban.	2001
Hamid Karzai is elected president by popular vote in Afghanistan's first democratic elections.	2004
Hamad Karzai is reelected.	2009

World History

1865	The American Civil War ends.
1879	The first practical lightbulb is invented.
1914	World War I begins.
1917	The Bolshevik Revolution brings communism to Russia.
1929	A worldwide economic depression begins.
1939	World War II begins.
1945	World War II ends.
1957	The Vietnam War begins.
1969	Humans land on the Moon.
1975	The Vietnam War ends.
1989	The Berlin Wall is torn down as communism crumbles in Eastern Europe.
1991	The Soviet Union breaks into separate states.
2001	Terrorists attack the World Trade Center in New York City and the Pentagon in Washington, D.C.
2004	A tsunami in the Indian Ocean destroys coastlines in Africa, India, and Southeast Asia.
2008	The United States elects its first African American president.

Fast Facts

Official name: Islamic Republic of Afghanistan

Capital: Kabul

Official languages: Pashto and Dari

Kabul

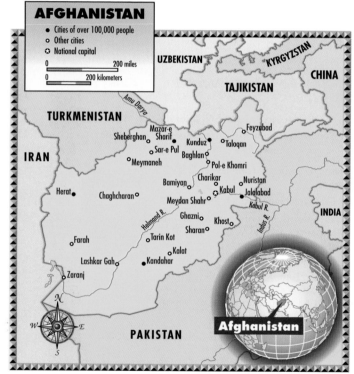

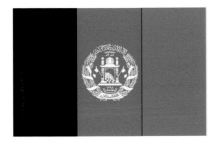

Official religion:	Islam
National anthem:	"Milli Surood" in Pashto; "Surood-e Milli" in Dari
Type of government:	Democracy
Chief of state:	President
Head of government:	President
Area:	251,825 square miles (652,225 sq km)
Widest point north to south:	About 350 miles (560 km)
Widest point east to west:	About 770 miles (1,240 km)
Bordering countries:	Turkmenistan, Uzbekistan, Tajikistan, and China to the north; Iran to the west; Pakistan to the east and south
Highest elevation:	Mount Noshaq, 24,557 feet (7,485 m) above sea level
Lowest elevation:	Amu Darya riverbed, 846 feet (258 m) above sea level
Longest navigable river:	Amu Darya, about 1,600 miles (2,575 m)
Average annual precipitation:	12 inches (30 cm)
Highest recorded temperature:	122°F (50°C) in Farah in August 2009
Lowest recorded temperature:	–62°F (–52°C) in Shahrak in January 1964

Bamiyan Valley

Minaret of Jam

Currency

National population (2009 est.): 28,396,000

Population of major cities (2006 est.):

Kabul	1,925,548
Kandahar	468,200
Herat	397,465
Mazar-e Sharif	375,181
Kunduz	347,450

Famous landmarks:

- ▶ *Blue Mosque,* Mazar-e Sharif
- ▶ *Friday Mosque,* Herat
- ▶ *Mosque of the Sacred Cloak,* Kandahar
- ▶ *Musallah Complex,* Herat
- ▶ *National Museum of Afghanistan,* Kabul

Economy: Afghanistan mines salt, natural gas, chromite, iron, copper, zinc, lead, gold, and silver. It also has rich deposits of amethysts, rubies, topazes, and lapis lazuli. Major agricultural products include wheat, cotton, rice, fruits, melons, and nuts. Afghans also raise goats, sheep, cattle, horses, and yaks. Textiles, especially carpets, as well as leather goods and metal products are manufactured there.

Currency: The afghani. In 2011, 45 afghanis = US$1.

System of weights and measures: Metric system

Literacy rate: 25% for women
55% for men

Schoolchildren

Dost Mohammad Khan

Common Pashto words and phrases:

As-salaamu' alaykum	Hello
Tsenga yee?	How are you?
Sheh yem	I am well
Luftan	Please
Tashakor	Thank you
Ta da kom zaee ye?	Where are you from?

Prominent Afghans:

Ahmad Shah Durrani   (ca. 1722–1773)
Founder of the Durrani dynasty

Kamal ad-Din Bihzad   (1455?–1536?)
Painter

Dost Mohammad Khan   (1793–1863)
Emir of Afghanistan

Hamid Karzai   (1957–)
President

Mullah Omar   (1959–)
Leader of the Taliban

Muhammad Zahir Shah   (1914–2007)
Last king of Afghanistan

To Find Out More

Books

- ▶ Downing, David. *Afghanistan*. New York: Marshall Cavendish, 2009.

- ▶ Fordyce, Deborah. *Afghanistan*. New York: Marshall Cavendish, 2011.

- ▶ Reedy, Trent. *Words in the Dust*. New York: Arthur A. Levine Books, 2011.

- ▶ Senzai, N. H. *Shooting Kabul*. New York: Simon & Schuster, 2010.

- ▶ Winter, Jeanette. *Nasreen's Secret School: A True Story from Afghanistan*. New York: Beach Lane Books, 2009.

Music and Video

- ▶ *Afghanistan: A Journey to an Unknown World*. Traditional Musicians. (CD). World Network, 2007.

- ▶ *Afghanistan: On Marco Polo's Road*. The Musicians of Kunduz and Faizabad. (CD). Multicultural Media, 1973.

- ▶ *Lost Treasures of Afghanistan*. (DVD). National Geographic Television & Film, 2006.

Web Sites

▶ **Afghanistan's Web Site**
www.afghanistans.com/
*For lots of background information
on Afghanistan and links to current
news stories.*

▶ **Homeland Afghanistan**
http://afghanistan.asiasociety.org
*To see videos about the history of
Afghanistan.*

▶ **My Afghan News**
www.myafghan.com/
For current news about the country.

Embassies

▶ **Embassy of Afghanistan**
2341 Wyoming Avenue, NW
Washington, DC 20008
202/483-6410
www.embassyofafghanistan.org

▶ **Embassy of Afghanistan
in Canada**
240 Argyle Avenue
Ottawa, Ontario K2P-1B9
613/563-4223
www.afghanemb-canada.net

Index

education and, 127
elections, 61, 65, 66, 67, 85, 90
executive branch, 61, *62*, 65, *65*, 66, 85
health care and, 126
House of Elders, 66, 67
House of the People, 66–67, 69
independence, 52
judicial branch, 65, 66, 69
laws, 53, 69
legislative branch, 53, 54, 65, 66–67, 69
loya jirga (council of chiefs), 48, 54, 64–65, *65*–66, 85, *85*
military, 50, 53, 56–57
National Assembly, 67
Northern Alliance, 57, 60, 61, 87
opium trade, 74
presidents, 61, *62*, 64, 65, *65*, 66, 67, *67*, 69, 85, 90, *90*
prime ministers, 54, 64
provincial governments, 66
shari'a law, 69
Supreme Court, 65, 69
Taliban, 22, 57–59, *58*, 60–61, 85, 88, 90, 103, 105, 108, 111, 115, 122, 125, 126, 133
treaties, 52, *52*, 53, 67
villages and, 119
women and, 66, *67*
graffiti art, 109
Great Britain, *19*, 48, 50, 51–52, *51*, 54
Great Game, 50–52

H

Habibullah Khan (emir), 50–51
hajj (fourth pillar of Islam), 101, *101*
Hazaragi language, 88
Hazarajat region, 88
Hazara people, 84, 87–88, *87*, 97, 122

Hazrat Ali (Islamic spiritual leader), 96, 97, 113
health care, 77, 125–126
Helmand River, 14, 15, 23, 81
henna parties, 121
Hephthalites. *See* White Huns.
Herat, 17, *17*, 31, 38, 44, 45, 46, 47, 61, 75, *76*, 81, 88, 90, 106, 107, 111, 112, *112*, 113–114, 115, 119
Herat Academy, 107
Himalayan Mountains, 8
Hinduism, 43, 44–45, 95, 97, 103
Hindu Kush mountain range, 8, 9, 15, 18–19, 20, 21, 30, 33, *33*, 77
historical maps. *See also* maps.
  Afghanistan (1500–1800), *48*
  Silk Road, *41*
holidays, 102–103, 126
horses, 29, 41, 45, 75, 91, 121, 124–125, *125*
Hosseini, Khaled, 115
House of Elders, 66, 67
House of the People, 66–67, 69
hydroelectric power, 80–81, *80*

I

'Id al-Adha holiday, 102–103
'Id al-Fitr holiday, 102, *102*
Imami Shia sect, 92
insect life, 28, *28*
Islam. *See also* religion.
  Aga Khan (spiritual leader), 92, 113
  animal sacrifices, 103, 121
  art and, 107
  communism and, 55
  conversions, 44–45, 97
  Cyrus the Great and, *37*
  Five Pillars of Islam, 99–101
  holidays, 102–103, *102*
  Imami Shia sect, 92
  Kushan Empire, *42*
  madrassas (religious schools), 58

minarets (mosque towers), 98, *98*, 112, *112*
mosques, 17, *17*, 75, 94, 97, *97*, 98–99, *98*, 111, 112, *112*, 113
muezzin (Islamic crier), 98–99, *99*
Muhammad (Islamic prophet), 44, 59, 95–96, 99
Mullah Omar, 57–58, 59, *59*, 85, 133
mullahs (religious leaders), 98, 99, 119, 121, 126
national flag and, 63, *63*
prayer, 69, 97, 98, 99, *99*, 100, *100*, 101, 103, 113, 120, 122
al-Qaeda and, 60
Qur'an (holy book), 96, *96*, 97, 99, 107, 121
shari'a law, 69
Shia Ismaili sect, 92, 97, 113
Shia sect, 84, 95, 96, 97, 113
Sunni sect, 84, 86, 89, 91, 95, 96–97, 113
Taliban and, 57–58, *59*, 60
Zoroaster (prophet), 37
Ismailis. *See* Shia Ismaili sect.

J

Jahani, Abdul Bari, 64
Jahan-Suz (Herat leader), 45
Jalalabad, 21, 38, 81, 119
Jami, Nur ad-Din Abd ar-Rahman, 114
Judaism, 95, 97, 103
judicial branch of government, 65, 66, 69

K

Kabul, 17, 20, 21, 38, 47, 48, 49, 50, 57, 59, 61, 68, *68*, 80, 81, 87, 88, 103, 108, *108*, 109, 111, 115, *116*, 119, *126*

Meet the Author

RUTH BJORKLUND GREW UP IN RURAL NEW ENGLAND, spending her childhood living in a house on a lake. It was a quiet place filled with diverse trees, wild animals, ducks, and migratory birds. She spent a lot of time hiking, reading, fishing and rowing her small boat. When she was twenty, she packed up her belongings and drove across the country to make a new home in the Pacific Northwest.

She graduated from the University of Washington with a degree in comparative literature and later earned a master's degree in library science. She worked for several years as a children's and young adult librarian in the King County and Kitsap County library systems. When she stayed home to raise her two children, she began writing books for young people on science subjects such as endangered animals, unusual pets, the planet Venus, anatomy, childhood diseases, and epidemics. She has

PHILIP KOSLOW earned his B.A. and M.A. degrees from New York University and went on to teach and conduct research at Oxford University, where his interest in medieval European and African history was awakened. The editor of numerous volumes for young adults, he is also the author of *El Cid* in the Chelsea House HISPANICS OF ACHIEVEMENT series and of *Centuries of Greatness: The West African Kingdoms, 750–1900* in the Chelsea House series MILESTONES IN BLACK AMERICAN HISTORY.

PICTURE CREDITS